D1040634

ALSO BY PHILIP TOSHIO SUDO

Zen Guitar

Zen Computer

philip toshio sudo

a fireside book
published by simon & schuster
new york london toronto sydney singapore

FIRESIDE
Rockefeller Center
1230 Avenue of the Americas
New York, NY 10020

Copyright © 1999 by Philip Toshio Sudo

First Fireside Edition 2001
FIRESIDE and colophon are registered trademarks of Simon & Schuster, Inc.
Designed by P.T.S.

Manufactured in the United States of America

1   3   5   7   9   10   8   6   4   2

The Library of Congress has cataloged the Simon & Schuster edition as follows:
Sudo, Philip Toshio.
Zen computer / Philip Toshio Sudo.
p.   cm.
Includes bibliographical references.
1. Computers — Psychological aspects.   2. Computers — Religious aspects — Zen
Buddhism.   I. Title.
QA76.9.P75S83   1999
004 — dc21   99-10493
CIP

ISBN 0-684-85409-0
0-684-85410-4 (Pbk)
For information regarding special discounts for bulk purchases, please contact
Simon & Schuster Special Sales at 1-800-456-6798 or business@simonandschuster.com

to Tracy,

Naomi,

and Keith,

and all those who climb the shoulders

0010110100011001101010101101101101010101101101101010101011
1001100010110110101011111101011011011101010100110110110
0000011011010101101011001010010100010010000010001000
1010110100010010101010001011011101010011111010101000
1010100010010100100010110111010101010100101001000100
0110001001010010001000100100010000010101110
1101101110101011011010101010001001010010001001000
0110111001010101010100010010100110010001110
100010010101100010100100110100000011111111111110
0010110010101011101010101101011111011011110
1011011010101011010101011101011010101110101011
1101010011010011001010101010100110101010110110110
1011010101101101010100010001101010101011101101
1011101010011011011101110101010101010101010010
0100001001011010111011011101010101000100001001001
0010100010010010001011011101110101010010010010001
1011101010011001110110111011010101010100010010001

ZC

Contents

Working With Zen Computer

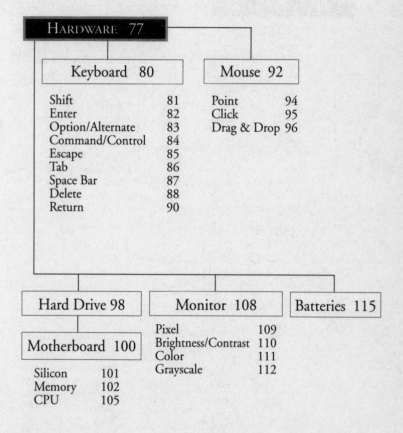

Working With Zen Computer

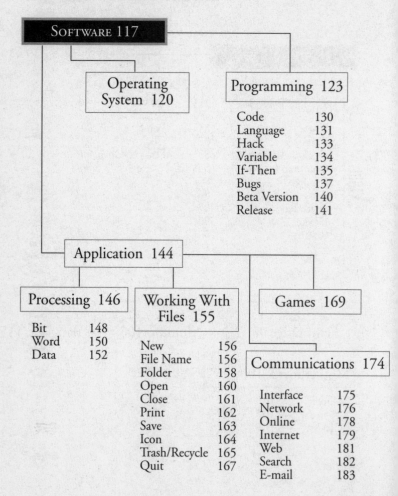

Read Me

Release Notes for Zen Computer, Version 1.0

T HANK YOU for choosing Zen Computer. May it give you a lifetime of good use.

This application marries the ancient principles of zen philosophy to the modern science of bits and bytes. Anyone who uses a personal computer can benefit, regardless of technical know-how. One run through the application and you'll never look at your computer in the same way again.

IN AN AGE of rapid technological advances, in which computers keep changing the way we work and play and even think, Zen Computer offers a way of living calmly amid constant upheaval. The very underpinnings of zen philosophy assume a world of continuous, unbroken change, in the cycles of day to night, season to season, birth to death. "You never step in the same river twice," goes the zen adage, for in zen thinking, everything flows and changes at every moment.

How to live with constant change, manage it, and deal with the fear it brings—especially if the change seems overwhelming, as it can today—lies at the heart of zen study, and thus, at the heart of Zen Computer.

Visionaries may paint a fantastical future driven by technology, a wired planet of cyberspace and virtual worlds with unprecedented access to information and knowledge. But cyberspace and virtual reality will offer no escape from the problems of the human heart. Information and knowledge will not supplant the need for wisdom. Rather than create a user-friendly virtual world, Zen Computer seeks to make a real world of friendly users.

Luddites fear that technology will dehumanize us, even enslave us, as we become increasingly dependent on machines for our way of living. That's all the more reason we need Zen Computer.

We lose our humanity when we become an extension of the machine—rigid in our thinking, unfeeling and uncaring, treating others as nameless, faceless numbers. We ignore common sense and begin uttering phrases like, "I can't deal with you because you're not in our computer," or, "The machine says the answer has to be this." We stop acting from the heart and start becoming drones.

Zen Computer is the antidote for those forces that make us drones.

Much as people may long to turn their backs on technology and return to a simpler life, in truth, we cannot retreat from technology anymore than we can unlearn how to split the atom. If we are to live in this brave new world and retain our humanity, our true battle lies not with technology, it lies within. There is where Zen Computer does its work.

We must accentuate the fact that we're *human* and that, as such, we differ from other species in three distinct ways:

- our communication skills
- our ability to use tools
- our self-awareness

Zen Computer seeks to cultivate all three qualities—improving our communications to promote better understanding, turning our use of tools into an art, raising our self-awareness. In short, Zen Computer views the computer as a means of elevating our humanity, not squashing it.

The computer is perhaps the most powerful tool ever put in the hands of the individual. Only the gun may rival it. But if the pen is mightier than the sword, then PCs should outperform the Uzi. Think of the personal computer's ability to amass and analyze information; present ideas in word, image, and sound; store, replicate, receive, and globally transmit those ideas instantly. These capabilities put enormous power in the hands of people. A lone voice can now communicate a message to thousands, even millions, with a few simple keystrokes, connecting with other computers in every corner of the globe.

Such power demands responsible use. Just as a gun can be put to ill purposes, so can a computer. There are people who would invade our privacy, spread untruths, embezzle money, even spread chaos by hacking into air-traffic control and other safety systems. Giving individuals more power does no good if they don't know the proper way to use it. Here is where Zen Computer offers a framework for living with such power.

For as much as technology transforms our lives and society, Zen Computer says true transformation—the kind that's authentic and profound—will not come through technology alone, but through people's souls. It says salvation arises from self-awareness, not better tools and faster communications; that world peace stems from inner peace; that freedom for all people first demands the self-discipline of each individual. *To cultivate self-awareness through the use of tools and communications*—this is the hard work Zen Computer seeks to support. Only then can we elevate our humanity.

Toward that end, the software in this package includes the following:

- The Seven Rules of Zen Computer
- A mindful way of looking at your machine

- Tips on responding calmly to program bugs and system crashes
- How to interface with people on the Internet and in the world at large

To install Zen Computer, read on.

System Requirements

I do not fear computers. I fear the lack of them.

—Isaac Asimov (1920–92)

Zen Computer works regardless of one's computer operating system or personal belief system. You need not belong to the church of Microsoft, worship at the altar of Apple, or convert to Buddhism to reap the benefits. You don't need to know about zen or even much about computers; just run through the application and zen will operate of its own course.

The only system requirement is an open mind. From there, everything follows.

. . .

IN A REVOLUTION as vast as the current technological one, it's easy to lose one's bearings. Some people may lose their jobs to a machine; others may have to acquire daunting new computer skills to keep up. The resulting upset can leave anyone feeling bewildered. Even leaders of the computer industry don't know where the technological revolution is heading; we all have to figure it out for ourselves. We need to stay open to change, to new ideas, to what's coming next.

Change creates opportunities for some and leaves others behind. Economically, it can divide the world into haves and have-nots. But on a spiritual level—the focus of Zen Computer—there are no have-nots. Spiritually, we all inherently *have*. We merely need to awaken to that fact. Every computer user and nonuser has the divine spirit within. If we're open to that realization and align ourselves accordingly, we begin the inner revolution that makes the outer computer revolution more profound.

Too many people get left behind in the computer revolution because their minds have closed. They're too set in their ways, too afraid to enter a realm in which they're ignorant and have to think new thoughts. They see themselves as smart, intelligent people and can't accept the feeling of not knowing. Or they think themselves too old or stupid to learn. "I haven't needed a computer before," goes the argument, "so why do I need one now?"

To an extent, they're right. Not everyone needs a computer.

In fact, we should all know how to function without one. But life is a process of transformation. In joining the computer age, we align ourselves with that process. What carries us through times of rapid change is the openness to learning and starting anew. Through not knowing, we learn humility. Through seeing the have-nots, we develop compassion. This is the revolution of mind Zen Computer seeks to enact.

An open mind will guide you far along the path of life, whatever your pursuit. We cannot know what lies in store or what doors may present themselves. Do we want to run from those doors? Get dragged through them? Freeze before them in fear? Or stride through them with open minds and open hearts, knowing that, in so doing, we stay on the true path, wherever it may lead. It's in our attitude toward change and opportunity that the future gets made.

The Japanese word for crisis, *kiki,* translates two ways: "danger occasion," but also "danger opportunity." In this thinking, every crisis creates an opportunity. The challenge is to see it. To do so, one has to have the right system requirements—a propensity to spy the glass half full, not half empty.

Kiki

Who can say when a door will open, or even what the door will look like? The great oceanographer Jacques Cousteau once said the pivotal moment in his life came when he broke his arm just as he was to test for entrance into the air force. Up until that point in his life, his dream had been to earn his pilot's wings, but the injury forced him to join the navy instead. That stroke of misfortune opened the door to his finding the love of his life, the sea.

The farther we go in life, the more we realize how events that seemed minor at the time—a chance meeting here, a left turn there—reveal themselves in hindsight to have dramatically altered the course of our lives. Who knows, this very day may yet reveal its significance to us years down the road. The future stretches out before us, uncharted. Find the open road and look back with a sense of wonder.

How pregnant this moment in time. How mysterious the path ahead.

Now, step forward.

FAQ Sheet

Computers are useless. They can only give you answers.

—Pablo Picasso (1881–1973)

M ANY PEOPLE are already applying zen in their lives, though they may not know it. We hear the word zen to-day in connection with things serene, enigmatic, minimal, aes-thetically clean, even fashionable. People like to say, "That's so *zen.*" But what exactly do they mean?

To ensure a common reference point, the following FAQ sheet offers some introductory background on zen—what it is, and what it isn't.

What is zen?

No one can say. Furthermore, anyone who proclaims an ability to answer in words is a fool. If someone asks, "What is zen?" the best answer may be a clap of the hands.

Hundreds of books, including this one, have been written about zen, but none can say what zen *is,* because zen can only be experienced. To ask, "What is zen?" is akin to asking, "What is music?" or "What is air?" Nothing we say can give us the actual experience of it. And yet the experience is there for everyone. Zen is like the punch line of a joke that makes you laugh; there's no conscious analysis of what makes it funny, just the spontaneous, natural reaction. The moment you start explaining the punch line to someone, the joke is lost.

The word *zen* is the Japanese pronunciation of the Chinese character *ch'an,* which itself is adapted from the Sanskrit word *dhyana,* meaning meditation or absorption. But zen has come to mean much more than meditation.

Zen

Zen is an awareness, a sensibility, a way of looking at things, a way of living life. Its way is to float like a ball on the river of life, right now, *in this moment,* aware of both the cosmic order and the tiniest detail; to coordinate mind, body, and spirit so as to express one's true nature in every action; to do what comes *naturally.* When the hand goes up automatically to catch a ball that's thrown unexpectedly, the action arises spontaneously, out of one's true nature, in the same way the fruit falls from the tree when it is ripe. This is zen action—catching without thought of "catching," doing without "doing." If it sounds simple, it is. But imagine carrying that naturalness through to every action. If it sounds difficult, it is that, too.

The route to this sort of naturalness lies in cultivating a quality of mindfulness.

What is mindfulness?

Mindfulness is simply maintaining a heightened presence of mind. Through sheer force of will, we turn our minds into their own disciplinarians, like the teacher in school yelling, "Pay attention!" Zen masters call it "minding mind." Pay attention to what you're doing *right now*; to how you're doing it; to the ways of nature and your place within it; to your heart, your body, your intuition, your very breath. Zen lies in all these things.

Some people may think that mindfulness sounds too self-absorbed. But zen requires a constant balancing act—to look deep inside ourselves while at the same time developing awareness of our environment and all our relations within it. The more mindful we are of what we do, the more mindful we are of each other. Zen demands balancing the paradoxical. Pay attention, zen says, but do not pay attention—that is, force yourself to pay attention to the point where you forget you're forcing yourself and simply start paying attention; only then will you know something about zen. Do without doing; expect the unexpected; pursue a goal without pursuing, with no goal in mind. Logically, these words make no sense. But in zen, truth lies beyond the grasp of logic, in the realm of intuition. A playwright once said, "The center of the contradiction—that's where you want to be." Zen lies there, balancing the opposites.

Is zen a religion?

No. But in learning to flow with the natural order of things, students of zen develop a profound sense of spirituality—an intuitive feel for the divine within nature's cycles and rhythms.

Some people mistake the spirituality of zen for religion. But zen worships no deity, follows no sacred text, and shuns dogma of any kind. (I make a distinction here between "pure" zen, which decries attachment to any system of understanding, and Zen Buddhism, which has formalized an approach to zen from a Buddhist context of structure and rules.) Rather than supplanting religious convictions, the spirituality one finds in zen can make one's existing faith even stronger. Thus, we hear people describe themselves as Zen Buddhists, Zen Christians, or even Zen Atheists.

If anything, zen adheres to the Chinese cosmology of yin-yang, symbolized by the interlocking fetal figures of black and white (see illustration).

What is yin-yang?

Yin and yang represent the pairs of opposites, born of the source of all things, that comprise our experience of the cosmos: life and death, day and night, matter and space, male and female, on and on. Zen represents the constant balancing of these elements, which are not conflicting but complementary—the two sides of one coin. One does not exist without the other, and within each fetal figure of the circle lies a small circle of the other. That is to say, there are circles within circles within circles, never in a state of perfect balance, but always changing, thus requiring an ongoing process to find the great Middle Way between the two.

Yin-yang

Zen Computer proposes that yin-yang lies even at the heart of computing, in the very nature of digital technology.

What characterizes digital technology is its ability to render, store, and transmit information in a binary system of 0s and 1s. Every keystroke or click of the mouse sends tiny on/off signals to the computer's transistors, which represent the signals as sets of 1s and 0s. Grouped together, these 1s and 0s, called *bits*, serve as the computer's internal language.

All languages have their poetry. The poetry of the binary language lies in its inherent yin-yang nature. In fact, the developer of the binary number system, German philosopher and mathematician Gottfried Wilhelm Leibniz (1646–1716), was inspired by yin-yang philosophy. He credits the classic Chinese text *I Ching* (The Book of Change) with having a profound impact on his thinking. By the end of his life, Leibniz had come to view 0 and 1 in zenlike terms, as part of the complex interaction of life and consciousness—1 representing God, he believed, and 0 representing the void.

Throughout Zen Computer, you'll see constant reference to this poetic interplay between 0 and 1, for these numbers carry symbolic importance in zen as well.

What do 0 and 1 represent in zen?

In zen, 0 is like the ocean and 1 is like a wave. A wave is of the ocean, but distinct from it, too. Each wave swells up out of the water and moves forward through space and time. The ocean, constant, manifests and powers the wave.

As human beings, we experience this ocean, this 0, like surfers—catching the wave, or 1, as it rises, and riding it until it dies out or we crash. Each wave, then, is like a lifetime; one ride over, we return to catch another. Throughout, we're always wet and in the water.

In zen calligraphy, brush masters use 0, or the circle, to represent a multitude of truths: the inexpressible level of understanding that lies beyond conceptualization; the principle of eternity, with no beginning and no ending; all the various cycles of life, from birth to death to the rhythm of the clock and the seasons; the fundamental power of circular and spherical energy in the physical world, with all things in constant circular motion.

Look at your computer. Is it moving? And your desk? Does it, too, move? On the largest level, the answer is always yes. Everything on this earth is always moving in a circle, as the world turns on its axis and orbits the sun at 60,000 miles an hour. These circles within circles energize our physical existence. In the very center lies the still point of the moving world, as at the eye of the tornado. The still point at the center is where Zen Computer leads.

Where do we find this still point of everything that moves? In mind, body, and spirit. A zen lesson designed to illustrate this notion tells of two monks arguing at a flagpole. One says, "The wind is moving." The other counters, "The flag is moving."

The master Bodhidharma, upon hearing the exchange, corrects them both. "Not the wind, not the flag," he says. "Mind is moving."

If mind is moving, Bodhidharma says, we are not calm and at the center.

Once we align ourselves through zen and stand at the center of the circle, we become like the surfer on the wave. Then the still point at the center moves as we move—moving according to movement, staying ever balanced, always finding equilibrium. As the masters say, the way is known through balancing, not balance.

All these ideas, zen masters express through 0.

OUT OF THE VOID of 0, the masters say, is born 1, the real world of matter, space, and time. This 1 represents the union of all things, as well as the linear nature of time. Everything in 1—the grass, the sea, you, me, the computer—is a manifestation of 0. In other words, 1 is not separate from 0, but rather the veil of 0, like the display monitor that masks the internal workings of the computer. Leibniz put it thus: "The soul is the mirror of an indestructible universe."

Even the Japanese and Chinese handwriting styles reflect the zen philosophy inherent in these numbers. In Western cultures, for example, the number 0 is generally written starting at the 12 o'clock position and proceeding counterclockwise back to the 12 o'clock position. In the handwriting of Japan and China, however, 0 is drawn starting at the 6 o'clock position and moving clockwise around to the 6 o'clock position again. This action emphasizes the feeling of arising out of nothing, moving through time, and returning to origin.

Westerners also write the number 1 differently, as a vertical line. One might see it depicting an individual standing. Handwriting styles in Japan and China, however, denote 1 horizontally rather than vertically, emphasizing the idea of movement through time, of a path beginning and ending.

The aim of Zen Computer will be to find the intuitive balance between 0 and 1—not the halfway point at 0.5, but that transcendent place where both $0 \neq 1$ *and* $0 = 1$, *and* where neither $0 = 1$ nor $0 \neq 1$.

How can 0 = 1?

Logically, of course, this makes no sense. It is a mathematical truth that zero cannot equal one.

In zen thinking, though, "nothing" is still "something." Sitting in meditation means doing nothing and something at the same time. Similar examples abound in everyday life. In politics, nonparticipation in the system still makes a political statement. In television, *Seinfeld* can famously proclaim itself to be about nothing, yet still find material for laughs.

Yes, zero does not equal one, but with the right perspective, zero *does* equal one. The aim of zen is to realize both truths simultaneously, in the same way we understand the truth in the saying, "The more things change, the more they stay the same."

I am not talking here about the kind of illogic portrayed in George Orwell's novel *1984*—a totalitarian world in which the state dictated "War is Peace," "Freedom is Slavery," and $2 + 2 = 5$. True zen manifests compassion, not oppression. Zen accepts the truth of $2 + 2 = 4$, while at the same time recognizing those instances where $2 + 2 = 5$—that is, where the whole of something exceeds the sum of its parts. Add two musical notes to another two and you get four musical notes. But put the right pairs together with the proper sense of space and time, and suddenly you get a fifth element—a beautiful melody with a power far beyond the individual character of each note. Therein lies zen.

AFTER READING this FAQ sheet, you may find yourself more puzzled than when you began. If you're confused, it only means your mind is trying to comprehend something. Relax and let your mind do its work.

As you proceed, you'll find plenty of moments when zen doesn't make sense and yet rings true. Whatever means we use to approach it, that unnameable thing we call *zen* always has been and always will be; it simply *is,* whatever name we give it. Clap your hands, laugh at a joke. Zen is to be found in every action and every thing—including the computer. The truth of zen is already known to you. All you need to do is realize it.

Zen Computer is here to help.

Boot

Out of nothing I have created a strange new universe.

—János Bolyai (1802–60),
Hungarian mathematician

I F YOU ARE READY to begin the application, it's time to turn on your computer—in computer jargon, to boot up. With the initial jolt of electricity, the computer starts preparing itself to get up and running, taking inventory of itself, setting switches, installing programs. In essence, the machine has to kick start itself, "pull itself up by its own bootstraps" before it can start working; hence the term *boot*.

Zen requires the same approach. No one can do the work of zen for you; you must pull yourself up by your own bootstraps and study zen yourself, the same way that only you can find the balance needed to ride your bicycle. Other people can describe the feeling to you and suggest ways to approach it, but ultimately, you have to learn it for yourself. Zen requires self-reliance.

With that in mind, prepare yourself to boot the machine, first by sitting at the computer, then starting.

Sitting at the Computer

People who do best on-screen are those who reflect on what they're doing.

—SHERRY TURKLE, PROFESSOR OF THE SOCIOLOGY OF
SCIENCE, MASSACHUSETTS INSTITUTE OF TECHNOLOGY

When you sit down at your computer terminal, be aware of your physical relationship to the machine. Zen practice seeks to coordinate body, mind, and spirit, so make yourself aware of your body and what it's doing. Like a concert pianist preparing to play, you must be relaxed and alert at the same time. Your chair, monitor, and keyboard should all be at the right height to avoid stress and strain. And in the words of parents throughout the ages: Sit straight.

There are practical reasons as well as philosophical ones for proper posture. According to the U.S. Bureau of Labor Statistics, repetitive strain injury—caused chiefly by computer use—is the leading occupational injury in America, affecting more than 300,000 people a year. Proper posture helps avoid such injury.

More important, proper posture reflects a disciplined state of mind. One can be a brilliant programmer while slouched in a chair; I've seen many people do this. But brilliant programming is not the same as self-discipline. To be *mindful* means to be aware not only of what we're doing, but *how* we're doing it. Through zen practice, we seek to put ourselves in mental, physical, and spiritual balance with the world. That balance should carry through in everything we do and every action we make, whether walking, standing, sitting, or lying down.

When we sit with proper posture, we put ourselves into—or, better yet, maintain—the desired state of physical balance. Physical practice helps develop our mental and spiritual balance. The brilliant programmer slouched in the chair may produce works of genius. But sustained poor posture is evidence that something in that person's life is off-center, either mentally, physically, or spiritually.

Of course, most of us tend to neglect our posture after working for awhile. Our bodies begin to slump, our eyes become tired, our thinking runs down a narrow track. Be mindful of these moments and make the necessary corrections—straighten up in the chair, or get up and take a break. In this way we realign ourselves and keep our minds on the present moment.

ASIDE FROM ASSUMING proper posture, Zen Computer also asks you to physically acknowledge the machine. Before you start and after you finish working, make this one simple gesture toward your computer: Give it a nod.

In the art of Japanese swordsmanship, the samurai bow to their swords before and after training. These bows are a way of acknowledging the sword's function and importance in life, and a recognition that using this tool is fundamentally a spiritual endeavor. Through hours and hours of perfecting their techniques, the samurai connect themselves with the principles that guide the universe—balance, harmony, the oneness of all things. They learn not only physical balance, but mental and emotional balance as well—when to fight, when not to fight, when to attack, when to turn the other cheek. They come to understand the fleetingness of life, knowing that a single sword stroke can fell a person, and so seek to maintain harmony by learning to resolve conflict without having to fight. They realize that, in battle, they and their opponents are not separate combatants so much as pairs of opposites linked in the dance of yin and yang that unites the universe. In samurai thinking, when the sword is in the hands, it houses the soul.

Zen Computer proposes that we regard the computer in the same way: to view work at the machine as part of spiritual training. In zen thinking, spiritual practice is not something confined to a place of worship; it is never ending. This practice must inform every part of the day, including all the hours we sit at the computer. Through Zen Computer, we begin to integrate our computer work with our spiritual life.

Some people might balk at the idea of showing respect to a machine. Doesn't that imply subservience, they ask? Besides, the machine acts so impetuously, who can respect it? Why show respect to something so arbitrary and unreliable?

Because it gives to us.

WHEN OUR TOOLS work, we take them for granted. They're functioning; that's what they're supposed to do. But when the computer crashes, the soldier's gun jams, or the car brakes fail, we realize the extent of our vulnerability. Indeed, we rely upon tools to give us something—a supercapability, a sense of security. When they fail, we want to lambaste them. Yet those are the moments we should acknowledge all the more what they mean to us.

For many of us, the computer is the means by which we earn a living. To give it a nod, then, is a way of thanking the tool for what it provides in life. It helps put bread on the table and a roof overhead. It gives us work and pleasure, exercises our minds, brings us information, connects us with other people. It is a partner helping us achieve our goals.

Nodding also thanks the unseen hands and minds who helped create our machine. The object sitting before us was not born on a store's shelf. It came from a line of scientists, engineers, inventors, programmers, mathematicians, designers, manufacturers, all of whom built on the knowledge of those who came before them. It came from makers of plastics and glass, from packers and shippers, from the workers who built roads and rails and airplanes, and all their parents who brought them into the world and the teachers who taught them what they needed to know. All of these people infuse each machine with their very spirit. By nodding, we thank these people for what they gave to make the tool in front of us.

If we learn to show respect this way, a psychological transformation can take place. The machine becomes less soulless. The sculptor Isamu Noguchi said something similar once in speaking about a series of stone works in his personal gallery. When visitors looked upon those stones in appreciation, he wanted them to feel as though the stones were looking back. The same feeling occurs when we nod to the computer. In giving it thanks, we become aware of the interplay between tool and user, between the animate and inanimate. Through this interplay, we recognize the interconnectedness—the oneness—of all things.

A famous story about Buddha tells of a time he gathered his monks for a speech. Wordlessly, he held up a flower. Only one in the crowd, Kasyapa, broke into a smile, understanding the master's message: The truth transcends words and forms. All things speak of God, be they flowers or stones or boxes of plastic, wire, and microchips.

If the Buddha held up a computer today, what would you do?

The challenge of zen is to adopt the attitude of nodding *toward everything*. If we're truly mindful, we begin to acknowledge the car for the role it plays in getting us from one place to another, the lightbulb for illuminating us in the dark, the icebox for preserving our food. We express gratitude for the telephone, the shovel, the pillow, the dish, the shower. Soon, we are thanking everything and each other.

Behold a better world.

Start

Breathe,
Breathe in the air.
Don't be afraid to care.

—PINK FLOYD'S
THE DARK SIDE OF THE MOON,
OFTEN HEARD IN COLLEGE COMPUTER LABS

F or most of us, turning on the computer is a routine act. Zen Computer asks that we make it a mindful one.

Each time we start the computer marks a new beginning. Even if we're applying ourselves to tasks left over from the day before, today's start is a new start—a chance to remind ourselves that, in this moment, we embark down the path of spiritual growth with a fresh step and a beginner's mind.

The beginner's mind is a mind free of preconceptions, arrogance, and cynicism. It is like an empty cup, ready at all times to receive a drop of wisdom.

The image of the empty cup stems from a classic zen parable, told and retold through the years, about the zen master

Nan-in. Nan-in was said to have received a university professor inquiring about zen. As the meeting progressed, the host noticed that the professor spent most of the time talking instead of listening. Nan-in began pouring the visitor's tea until it overflowed onto the table.

"What are you doing?!" the professor exclaimed.

"Like this cup, you are full of your own ideas," the master said. "How can I teach if you don't first empty your cup?"

Every time we start up the computer, we should remember to empty our cup. Whatever pressures we feel, whatever carries over from the previous day's work, whatever challenges lie ahead, we must remember to empty our cup and start fresh. This is mindful thinking.

On many computers, we hit the on/off button and the machine chimes, indicating that it's on. Use this chime as a reminder, the way some people tie a string around a finger. When you hear the chime, empty your cup.

The way to empty your cup is to practice the most important thing you'll ever do in life:

Breathe.

BREATHING is central to all zen practice. It initiates our life outside the womb, and continues in and out like the tide until the moment we die. The simple act of inhale/exhale gives life a fundamental rhythm, and reminds us of the interplay between yin and yang.

Most of us never give breathing a second thought. But Zen Computer asks that you stop and consider your breath each time you start the machine. When you hear the start-up chime, sit straight, plant your feet on the ground, and take a slow, deep breath. If you wish, close your eyes. Inhale through your nose and exhale through your mouth. Imagine your body filling up like an air tank, from the bottom of your feet to the top of your head. As you exhale, imagine the tank emptying, all the way to the bottom. Do this ten times before you begin your work.

Count each breath. Make them as slow and long as you can without straining, and do not rush yourself, especially as you approach breaths nine and ten. To the end, stay focused on the act of breathing *to the exclusion of everything else.*

If you haven't tried this before, you'll find it's easier said than done. The harder you focus on breathing, the more you'll notice stray thoughts roaming through your mind. These thoughts may even sound like incessant chatter. Let the chatter come and go. Refocus yourself, and continue where you left off.

With practice, slow, deep breathing should begin to quiet the mind and induce a sense of calm. We're often reminded to "take a deep breath and count to ten" when we become angry. Slow, deep breathing has a physiological effect on the body, returning it to an equilibrium, coordinating body, mind, and spirit. Control your breathing and you control yourself—especially in times of panic or crisis.

Regular, practiced breathing also develops self-discipline.

None of us really needs to "practice" breathing because it occurs naturally, but by consciously focusing on this natural act, we impose discipline on our minds and bodies, and so further our spiritual development.

To GUIDE YOUR breathing in the initial stages of practice, you may use the number keys along the top row of your keyboard. You can begin by gazing at the number 1 key, doing a long, slow inhale, then a long, slow exhale. Proceed to the number 2 key and repeat. On the tenth breath, finish by looking at the number 0 key. Again, do not rush a single breath.

Through these ten breaths, you span the entire range of the zen and digital universe—from 1 to 0. With your first breath, you empty your cup and enter the world at 1 with your beginner's mind, realizing the unity of all things. With your last breath, you empty your cup at 0, contemplating the inexpressible mystery of the Great Void.

Meditate on these ten keys and, after a while, your attention naturally turns to the symbols at the top of each key. On many machines, they look like this:

$$! \quad @ \quad \# \quad \$ \quad \% \quad \^{} \quad \& \quad * \quad (\quad)$$
$$1 \quad 2 \quad 3 \quad 4 \quad 5 \quad 6 \quad 7 \quad 8 \quad 9 \quad 0$$

Consider the following Ten Points of Meditation:

Ten Points of Meditation

A t 1, you may see **!** and think of it as a riding crop, spurring on your spirit: *Awaken! Do it! Now! This moment!*

AT 2, you may see the **@** symbol and contemplate where you're "at" in this moment: physically in relation to your machine, your environment, and the constellation of the universe; mentally in the clarity or confusion of your mind; spiritually on your path of growth. Or you may see yourself inside a circle—at the center of the cosmos, with all the heavens surrounding you as though you were a babe in the womb.

AT 3, you may see the **#** sign and think of your place among the infinite multitudes in the universe, from every grain of sand to every star in the sky. Or you may view the **#** sign as a crossroads, knowing you choose your own path and live with your decisions every day. Or you may picture a tic-tac-toe board and think of all the moves that have brought you to this point in life, realizing that the only opponent you'll ever face lies within.

AT 4, you may contemplate the **$** sign and think hard about your feelings toward money. How important is it to you? What role does it play in your life? How much do you need? How much do you give? Are you thankful for what you have?

Imagine that penny in your pocket, with its date, 1959. How many hands has it passed through? What has it bought, provided? Where was it lost, and found, along the way? How far has it traveled to reach you? That one coin connects you to all that has gone before, and all that is to come. Whom will it go to next? What will it buy?

At 5, you may meditate on the % sign and ask yourself, am I giving 100 percent? You may also think of the indivisibility of the universe—that from beginning to end, there are no percentages. All is zero over zero.

At 6, you may gaze upon the ^ symbol and think of the roof over your head that shelters you from storm. Or maybe you see an arrow pointing upward, showing the way for your spirit. Or you may see a mountain: Imagine yourself as large as Mt. Fuji, sitting in your chair, serene and immovable. Consider how you endeavor to climb the spiritual mountain, choosing your own path step by step, upward toward the sky.

At 7, you may regard the & symbol and dwell on all the things that link us—you and I and she and he and water and soil and heaven and earth, going back through time and generations. There is never an end to "and"; it leads infinitely to the Great

Void. Or you may look upon **&** as a pictogram of someone sitting, back to a mountain, contemplating star and moon, inhaling the whole of the night, exhaling the sky.

At 8, you may view the * sign and think of that star shining down from far away, sharing a relationship with you in this gigantic universe. What do you wish upon when you see it? You may also regard the * as a footnote, reminding you to empty your cup and return to the beginner's mind.

At 9, you may contemplate the (symbol and think of opening something new in life, starting now with your beginner's mind. Or you may envision a crescent moon ending its cycle, reflecting on the passage of time, the cycle of the seasons, and the cycle of life and death.

At 0, you may see the) symbol and think of closure, making peace with yourself or letting go of something that was never yours to hold. Or you may think of the moon beginning its cycle again, reflecting on the signs of rebirth inherent in all of nature.

Every time you turn on the computer, take ten deep breaths and consider these Ten Points of Meditation. When you sit down at your machine in the morning, breathe. When your computer crashes and you have to restart, breathe. At every moment, breathe and give thanks for the air. For what is your life but this very breath?

Now, sit straight and turn on the machine. Hear the chime and breathe ten times from 1 to 0. You are ready to install the Seven Rules of Zen Computer.

Install

The Seven Rules of Zen Computer

Each problem that I solved became a rule which served afterwards to solve other problems.

—RENÉ DESCARTES (1596–1650),
FRENCH PHILOSOPHER, SCIENTIST, MATHEMATICIAN

T HE MORE WE perceive the world to be rapidly changing around us, the more we require an inner sense of balance. When change feels overwhelming, we have to find the place that is unchanging, the still point amid turbulent movement.

The Seven Rules of Zen Computer will help guide you to that point. Let them serve as your support system when working at the computer, and guide your thinking away from it as well. Return to them when feeling lost amid constant change, for they can restore your center.

A warning, though: There is an exception to every rule. Do not cling to what's written here, for the way to zen is through letting go. Absorb the Seven Rules like the artist who learns the rules of painting, knowing that true art comes from throwing them all away. Ultimately, you must get to the point where the rules become so internalized that you go on to transcend them.

THE SEVEN RULES OF ZEN COMPUTER:

1. Expect the unexpected.
2. It always takes longer than you think.
3. Do not waste time.
4. Learn and teach, teach and learn.
5. Warm heart, cool head.
6. Do good work.
7. Know when to turn the machine off.

Proceed with your installation.

❖

1. Expect the unexpected.

*There's going to be a bunch of new problems
that nobody's even imagined.*

—BRUCE STERLING, SCIENCE-FICTION WRITER,
AUTHOR OF *THE HACKER CRACKDOWN*

Anyone who has used computers more than casually knows the frustration of losing a crucial file, watching the system crash in mid-operation, or having data corrupt for no apparent reason. I remember working for a daily newspaper once, in the early days of computers, with a room full of reporters trying to finish their stories for the evening deadline. Suddenly the power surged. All the screens flashed, then froze. An uproar ensued. Half the staff, including me, hadn't saved their stories. Ten minutes to deadline and all our work gone. We banged on our terminals and screamed, but we had to start over.

No one wants to be reminded at ten minutes to deadline, but the unexpected occurrence is what brings us back to the present moment. If we lose something we've taken for granted, we're suddenly made aware of its value. If we're presented with a crisis, we're forced to act on it right now. Zen is what helps us to live in the present moment mindfully—to avoid panic and keep composure, to be thankful for what we have and maintain some perspective.

That computer file you lost may seem like the most important thing in the world to you at ten minutes to deadline. But the mind is narrow at that point. What if in the next moment you received a phone call telling you a loved one had just died? How important would that file seem?

To expect the unexpected means to recognize the potential for sudden, unpredictable change, whether it's a computer crash, a car crash, or a plane crash. This does not mean we go around expecting the worst; rather, *we take nothing for granted.* When we take things for granted, we're unprepared for loss or crisis or anything out of the routine. Yes, we may remember to save an important computer file, but how many of us remember to save money for that proverbial rainy day? How many of us complain about our jobs, until we see a friend get laid off? How many of us remark at the death of a loved one, "I never got a chance to tell her . . ."?

We even take our own breath for granted, ignoring the reality that one day it will end. Death is inevitable, yet it usually comes unexpectedly. Live life here and now, with gratitude for what we have, and there will be no regrets.

The way to expect the unexpected is not to expect anything.

❖

2. It always takes longer than you think.

The way to stay on schedule is to make another one.

—Ed Rasala, computer engineer,
Data General Corp.

The writer Douglas Hofstadter, author of *Gödel, Escher, Bach: An Eternal Golden Braid,* coined what he calls "Hofstadter's Law":

It always takes longer than you expect, even when taking into account Hofstadter's Law.

No matter what kind of system we have or what the application is, nothing in computer work seems to go as quickly as we think it should. The faster computers move, the more they try our patience. We get a more powerful machine and it still doesn't process fast enough to satisfy us. Simple as a task might seem to finish, it inevitably takes longer than predicted.

There's always one more thing to get right, to tweak, to test again. On the umpteenth "last run-through," something still doesn't work or another niggling problem crops up that demands our attention. We plow ahead, our train of thought locked on a track, glancing at the clock in disbelief. We can be tidying up a small file or readying a new product for the marketplace—it always takes longer than we think.

The same law applies to our spiritual development. Hard as we might work at it, spiritual growth doesn't conform to a schedule. Answers don't come easily; sometimes, they don't come at all. The only way to deal with that frustration is to persevere and cultivate patience. In zen, nothing is ever rushed or hurried. Be it computer programming or seeking the truth, if we try too hard and rush toward a conclusion, more problems result.

Consider the parable about an eager young student who approached a master to learn the art of swordsmanship:

"Master," he said, "if I study diligently, how long will it take me to learn the art of swordsmanship?"

"Ten years, perhaps."

"What if I work exceptionally hard? Then how long will it take me?"

"Probably thirty years."

The student was perplexed. "I'm willing to endure any hardship and make any sacrifice," he said. "I just want to learn the art in the shortest time possible."

"In that case," the master said, "it will probably take seventy years."

Perseverance is essential in zen practice; no one progresses without an effort of will. But the more we seek to hasten spiritual growth, the slower we proceed. Too much focus on where we want to be removes the focus from where we are. Just persevere right now. If you are doing all you can, that's all you can do. Perseverance begets patience; patience begets calm.

We can practice patience anywhere. When we find ourselves sitting in traffic or riding the subway, glancing at our watch every ten seconds and tapping our feet impatiently, we can say to ourselves: *I'll get there when I get there. Looking at the watch won't make me go any faster.* The moment we become aware of checking the clock is the time to straighten our spines and take ten slow, deep breaths.

Even then, we still have to deal with other people's impatience, be they bosses, clients, or co-workers. We live in a society that demands instant gratification, and people are conditioned to getting what they want now, without having to wait.

Sometimes there's nothing you can do but suffer the wrath of others; that's life. Let them lose their patience. So long as you persevere on the path of zen, you will not lose your own. Remember, in times of tension, calm people have a calming effect on others. Be the yin of softness to the other's tempest yang.

We have to deepen our sense of rhythm, for the experience of Hofstadter's Law means we are out of sync with the natural order. Align yourself with the true pace of life. If you plant a seed today, don't ask for a garden overnight. A flower grows when it grows. Likewise, when you're installing a new system, preparing a file, or writing a new program, make sure to give yourself time.

Then prepare to give more.

3. Do not waste time.

Computers make it easier to do a lot of things, but most of the things they make it easier to do don't need to be done.

—ANDY ROONEY, HUMORIST

Have patience, but don't waste time. All we have in this life is right now—this breath. What's past is past, the future unknown. Through zen, we come to realize that every moment is precious, a unique chance for enlightenment. So, let no moment go to waste. Live mindfully at all times, wasting not a second.

We can be waiting for others to deliver their work, sitting on hold while calling for technical support, or stuck in an airport waiting for a storm to pass. Read. Write a letter. Or just sit and breathe.

If your computer crashes and you lose a half day's worth of work, does that half day go to waste? Not if you learn something from the experience that you can take with you. Refusing to waste time is an attitude—a commitment to make something of every moment. No one wants to redo half a day's work. But if it becomes necessary, we may gain some insight, provided we're of a mind to look for it.

With its games, chat rooms, and potential for endless Web surfing, the computer can be a giant sinkhole of time. A friend of mine once got so caught up in a computer game he lost track of time—an experience common to many users of the machine, regardless of the application. My friend started his game after breakfast and went straight through lunch. Soon it was twilight, then nightfall.

Around midnight, he thought, *I've wasted a whole day playing this stupid game.*

One could argue that my friend was pursuing the path of mastery, spending hours to excel at the game. But the true path of mastery involves self-mastery—to be free from obsession and able to control one's impulses. In contrast, my friend admitted that for the first time, he understood the feeling of having an addiction. Once he started the game, he said, he could not stop.

From that day forward, he decided never to play another computer game. "If I see a game and it looks cool, I won't even go near it," he said. "I know I'll get caught up in it and I can't afford the time." Having gained such insight about himself, who can now say he wasted his day playing a computer game?

Not wasting time does not mean every moment has to be productive. We may choose to spend time watching TV, surfing the Web, or shooting the breeze at work. So long as we do so mindfully—aware of our choice and giving of our time—we should feel no guilt.

It's your life. Spend your time the way you want to. But do so knowing what you do.

4. Learn and teach, teach and learn.

In times of profound change, the learners inherit the earth, while the learned find themselves beautifully equipped to deal with a world that no longer exists.

—ERIC HOFFER (1902–83),
AUTHOR, *THE TRUE BELIEVER*

computer makers like to talk about the machine evolving into just another appliance in our lives, as easy to use as a toaster or refrigerator. However, the fact remains that no one can just plug in a computer and go. Whether we're buying a computer for the first time, installing a new piece of software, or learning a new programming language, usage requires a lot of instruction and, typically, technical support as well.

Anyone who's tried to learn a new computer skill knows the frustration of talking to techies whose knowledge of computers is so advanced they can't seem to communicate it in layman's terms. And anyone who's ever tried teaching computer skills to a novice knows the frustration of talking to someone who can't seem to grasp what you're saying.

Part of the problem is linguistic: *Webster's Dictionary of Computer Terms* contains more than 7,000 computer-specific entries. Any conversation involving computers requires at least a minimum knowledge of this jargon and terminology. Even beginners have to know RAM from ROM and hard drive from software. So, to a certain extent, one has to be "bilingual" when entering the world of computers. We can't learn the skills without learning the language; conversely, we can't teach the skills without teaching the language.

Both sides need commitment. The student must make a commitment to learn; the teacher must make a commitment to teach. If one side fails on that account, the other side suffers.

I remember entering journalism school at the dawn of the computer age, when word processors were first becoming widespread. Every newsroom in the country had installed a word processing system, revolutionizing the way in which newspapers were written, edited, and laid out. But my particular journalism school still required students to write their stories on manual typewriters. For years, the school had refused to make the transition to computers—not for budgetary reasons, but because the teachers opposed it. Why? Because installing computers meant the teachers would have to learn the new system right along with the students, and they didn't want to do it.

Zen Computer will not function unless its users make a commitment to learn and teach, teach and learn throughout their lives—to maintain an empty cup to the very end. The moment we lack such a commitment, we step off the path of growth. As stated earlier, too many people seem unwilling to enter the computer age, not because they lack intelligence, but because they cannot empty their cup of ego and say, "Please teach me."

None of us is ever exclusively a student or a teacher. We are always both at the same time, and must always think of ourselves as such. A teacher can get you started on computers, but no one can teach you everything you need to know. At a certain point, you must teach yourself through trial and error, looking over other people's shoulders, putzing around, figuring out what methods work best for you. The same is true in life. A teacher can guide you, but in the end, you have to make your own way.

As you figure things out on your own, you share what you've

learned with others. This is the Japanese idea of the *sensei*. We often see the word translated as "teacher" in English, but literally it means "one who has gone before." In that regard, we are all senseis to somebody.

Sensei

Zen masters say, "When the student is ready, the teacher will appear." This means two things: When you're ready to learn, all things appear before you as teachers. And when you're ready to teach, the teacher within you appears. The more you recognize the help you've received from those who gave ahead of you, the easier it becomes to give of yourself to those coming up behind.

Mindful of this dual role, here are a few last words on learning and teaching.

In learning:

Show up.

If the teacher is there, you should be, too. Too often we make excuses as to why we can't show up—we're too busy, we don't feel like studying today, we'll go next time. There is no next time. There is only now.

Pay attention.

Show up not only in body, but in mind and spirit as well. Many times we're there, but not all there.

Climb on the shoulders of the teacher.

Look for ways to build on what exists. Advance so that humanity as a whole will benefit.

IN TEACHING:

Teach what you have learned.

Repay your debt to your teachers by bringing up those behind you. Lift them onto your shoulders.

Spare no effort when the student wants to learn.

If one method of teaching doesn't work, try another. Learn to impart the same lesson from different angles. Some teachers know the material but lack the method or communications skills to pass it on. To connect, they need to think outside themselves, think like others think, know how others learn. Remember, the teacher advances by advancing the student.

Pace the student.

Push when necessary, ease off when necessary. No one can learn everything well at one time, but high standards can help the student overachieve. As the philosopher John Stuart Mill once said, "A pupil from whom nothing is ever demanded that he cannot do, never does all he can." The best effort is expected, not nurtured.

Above all, deliver this simple message: You can do it.

Too many people believe they can't when they can. Stick with them and show them how. Once, during a meditation retreat, a student said to the zen teacher Soen Nakagawa, "I am very discouraged. What should I do?"

Soen replied, "Encourage others." This is zen thinking.

Learn and teach, teach and learn. There is nothing more fundamental in leading the enlightened life.

5. Warm heart, cool head.

*People chide one another; others complain;
leaders calm things down.*

—Esther Dyson, founder,
EDventure Holdings

There are certain computer users who call a technical support person and vent all their frustrations as though that person is personally responsible for whatever's wrong.

There are certain computer companies that care only about making a sale, then ignore the customer once problems arise after the sale has been made.

There are certain Internet users who go so far as to vandalize other computers, threaten other users, and even prey on children.

In life, as in the computer world, the daily course of human behavior ranges from the extremes of hotheaded to cold-hearted. The aim of Zen Computer is to adjust the internal thermostat so as to cool down the head and warm up the heart.

Whether in the business world or on the street, the competitive nature of life makes confrontation unavoidable. However, we must choose our battles wisely. How many people have fired off an angry memo in response to a perceived slight, only to regret their words a day later? When the blood begins to boil, breathe in slowly and deeply. In the end, the coolest head prevails.

Once, a student who claimed to have an uncontrollable temper approached the zen master Bankei, asking what to do about his rages. Bankei said, "Let me see this temper of yours." The student replied that he couldn't just show the master his temper on demand. "Then it must not be your true nature," Bankei said. "If it were, you could show it to me at any time. When you were born, you did not have it, and your parents did not give it to you." The lack of a cool head, in Bankei's eyes, showed a lack of self-mastery.

Samurai lore tells the tale of a swordsman sent to avenge the killing of his lord. At the moment the samurai cornered his foe, the opponent spit in his face. The samurai sheathed his sword. Had the samurai proceeded to kill at that point, the story goes, it would have been out of anger. Demanding control of himself, the swordsman put away his weapon until ready to act out of a coolheaded sense of duty.

Challenging as it may seem, keeping a cool head is easy compared with keeping a warm heart. So often we get wrapped up in our own problems and point of view. We lose the capacity to empathize. Armchair psychologists tell us our modern, technological society has become too rootless to care for community, too anonymous to recognize our common humanity, too cutthroat to feel compassion. Zen practice is a constant struggle to rise above these tendencies.

Indeed, zen masters say the highest achievement in zen is not to attain enlightenment, but to attain enlightenment and then "mingle with the people of the world"—to participate with others in their daily sorrows and struggles. For the very word *compassion* means "to suffer with." All people suffer in one way or another, no matter what their job title, income level, age, race, ethnicity, or domain name. When we share in the suffering of others, we break down our notions of separateness and begin to realize the zen principle that all is truly one—that, in the words of songwriter John Lennon, "I am he as you are he as you are me and we are all together."

No matter what crises arise at your computer, no matter what bug hits or who sends a flaming e-mail, keep your heart warm and your head cool. Zen Computer will not function otherwise.

6. Do good work.

*The real end of science is the honor
of the human mind.*

—CARL JACOBI (1804–51),
GERMAN MATHEMATICIAN

t a recent trade show, a major computer manufacturer spoke glowingly about his company's updated operating system. "It fixes a zillion bugs from the last one, of course," he said.

To take as given that the previous version, highly touted and widely sold in its own right, would contain a "zillion" bugs reflects what some computer analysts call a mindset of settling for work that's good enough—good enough to get by for now until updated later. In the interim, let the customer deal with the problems.

Competition and time pressure may necessitate a good-enough approach to getting products out the door. However, there is a difference between doing the best job one can do under a given set of circumstances, and just plain shoddy work. Too often, it seems, computer problems result from an indifference to good work—a lack of care about the job, the product, or the customer.

Mindfulness demands attention to every detail. What are we *doing?* Why? How? For whom? The clearer the answers to these questions, the higher the quality of our work. In every undertaking, our care shows through, whether we're working on something as big as a major new product or a task as simple as cleaning our desk. One mistake in a line of code can throw a whole program out of whack. One typo or spelling mistake in a document can raise doubts about the entire work.

I had a writing teacher once who automatically docked one grade for every spelling mistake she found in a story; three mistakes were an automatic F. Computerized spellcheckers offered no safety; after all, the sentence, "I red this book," would pass. In this teacher's mind, spelling mistakes were signs of laziness— a failure to read through one's own work carefully. If we as writers didn't read our own work carefully, the teacher said, why should any reader?

Admittedly, practical considerations sometimes require settling for less than what we know to be achievable. But whatever the constraints, we still do the best we can. It's when we give a halfhearted effort, cut corners, or phone in a performance that we need to ask ourselves why. Why waste the precious time of life doing something we don't care about? At the computer or in daily life, anything less than our best means we're off the path of zen—doing something against our essence and inner nature.

Do good work, too, in a moral sense—in the service of something larger than yourself. With the proper attitude, any form of work can serve the greater good, helping build a sense of community, advance a worthy cause, or uplift the human spirit. There is good work to be found even in the friendly phone manner of a technical-support person.

To do good work requires mindfulness in every moment— to be constantly vigilant of both effort *and* intention. Maybe you're praying for delivery of your product to retailers by Christmas. Or maybe you're praying for deliverance. Either way, the question is:

Have you done good enough work?

7. Know when to turn the machine off.

*The attention span of a computer
is only as long as its electrical cord.*

—POSTED ON THE INTERNET
AS "TURNAUCKA'S LAW"

In every office lives the Last Person Out the Door, the worker who always stays late and works weekends trying to make a deadline or catching up on things. Too often, it's because this person has no life outside work—no social life, no family life, nothing to go home to. A vicious cycle ensues as the more one works to avoid the emptiness, the less time remains to build a life outside of work.

We see the same thing happening with many young people sitting at their computers hour after hour, playing computer games, surfing the Web, chatting online, never venturing outside their room. They don't know when to turn the machine off.

In short, they need to get a life.

The computer can fill our lives with many things, even give life its meaning, but too much time at the machine indicates a life out of balance. Technology can stimulate our minds, dazzle our senses, and introduce us to people in all parts of the world, yet for all the flash of video games and friends in cyberspace, we cannot long ignore the demands of our physical bodies—the need to get about and stroll along the beach or boardwalk, to share in human contact. From the moment we're born, we need the touch of another to survive. The body longs for it; we damage ourselves the longer we ignore it. "Eat when hungry, sleep when tired," goes the zen adage. That is, follow the natural rhythms of the body, and you follow the path of zen.

Knowing when to turn the machine off means more than building a life away from the computer. In this technological age, we must also know when to turn the machine off when life is over. Medical science can now keep people alive indefinitely with life-support systems. On both a personal and societal level, we need to know when to turn the machine off—to let go of our attachment to life when it becomes pointless to hold on. Here, too, zen can show the way.

To understand the nature of death is to understand the nature of life; the two exist in an interplay of yin and yang. In zen, the passage from womb to tomb is a process of learning both how to engage in the world and disengage from it—how to live and how to die, how to cope with death and face the fear of it.

Life is always on the point of death, one accident away. We try to ignore that fact, yet we're reminded of it when we hear soldiers, survivors, and thrill-seekers say the moment of imminent death is when they feel most intensely alive. The Buddha tells a parable to make the same point. He describes a man chased by a tiger across a field to a precipice. Catching hold of a root, the man swings down over the edge, only to see another tiger waiting down below. Two mice, one white and one black, start gnawing at the vine.

"In this dire state," the Buddha says, "the man sees a luscious strawberry near him. Holding the vine with one hand, he plucks the strawberry with the other. How sweet the taste!"

The Buddha's lesson is to treat every moment the same way: to see the luscious strawberry and taste its sweetness. When death lurks at any moment, every breath becomes precious. If we can breathe that way, with that level of realization, we begin the move toward transcending life and death. We come to identify ourselves as the flame and not the candle. A candle may burn itself out. But fire is elemental, an energy that simply *is*.

BUILD A FULL LIFE, away from the machine as well as at it.

Burn brightly.

When it is time, take your leave.

Now 1.

Now 0.

Hardware

The real problem is not whether machines
think but whether men do.

—B. F. SKINNER (1904–90)

N OW THAT YOU'VE INSTALLED the Seven Rules of Zen Computer, you're ready to use the application. Here you will learn to view the hardware and software of your machine in a mindful way.

Computer hardware consists of things you can touch—things that exist physically in the world, with form and shape. In contrast, software exists only as invisible bits of information. Together, hardware and software comprise the yin and yang of computing—separate yet intertwined, each needing the other to function.

As humans, we tend to think of our "hardware," our physical body, as somehow separate from our "software," our mind and spirit. But, like the computer, the two are not two. They are one, designed to work in unison.

Remember: All is 1 is 0.

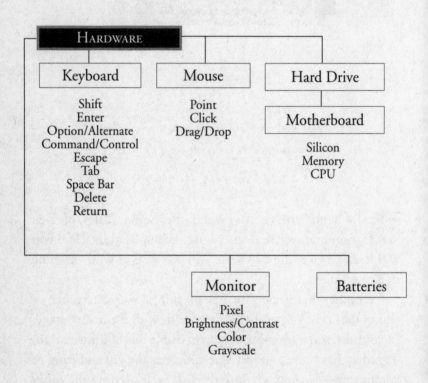

▽ 🗀 HARDWARE
  ▽ 🗀 Keyboard
    📄 *Shift*
    📄 *Enter*
    📄 *Option/Alternate*
    📄 *Command/Control*
    📄 *Escape*
    📄 *Tab*
    📄 *Space Bar*
    📄 *Delete*
    📄 *Return*

Keyboard

Press any key to start.

The keyboard, along with the mouse, is where we make bodily contact with the machine—where we establish a physical relationship. Just as a trumpet becomes the extension of the musician's body or a scalpel becomes the extension of the surgeon's, so should we view the computer as an extension of our own body. The keyboard is the primary means by which we implement the tool, express our will, and remake the world around us.

The first time we take up typing, we tend to feel awkward. Our fingers move deliberately over the keys as the mind consciously directs them, hunting and pecking for letters and symbols. With practice and time, though, we become so adept that fingers move over the keys unconsciously, automatically. Our hands develop their own intelligence. Remember this feeling— it is the essence of mind-body coordination. Whether driving the car, hitting a golf ball, playing the guitar—whatever you do—the feeling should be the same: effortless and flowing, without mediation of the mind. To carry that feeling throughout our lives is the ultimate state of mindfulness, because it means we always know what we're doing, without having to think about it.

Shift

Raise your sail one foot
and you get ten feet of wind.

—CHINESE PROVERB

The SHIFT key on the keyboard raises lower case to upper case. We endeavor to raise our awareness in the same way. Through practice, effort, and mindfulness, we experience a shift of consciousness. We pick up a handful of earth and see it as Earth; we scoop up a cup of water and see Water; we breathe in the air and think Air.

Excited as we may be to reach the point where our consciousness becomes Consciousness, we remain humbled by the fact that most of the time, we live in the lower case, only occasionally moving to the upper realm. This humility keeps us grounded.

BEWARE OF ANYONE WHO TALKS LIKE THIS ALL THE TIME—no one who truly understands the upper realm need continually scream for attention, be it a poet, preacher, or protester.

A single shift can raise your consciousness forever. The change is at your fingertips.

Enter

What is now proved was once only imagin'd.

—William Blake (1757–1827)

The ENTER key reminds us of a saying in the zen arts, "Enter by form, exit from form."

On one level, the saying guides us through the progression of artistry. It says, learn the formal rules of an art first, then throw them out in order to make an individual expression. Picasso had to paint the classical figure before he developed cubism. Charlie Parker had to learn the rules of harmony before he played bebop. In the same way, we have to learn the rules of computers—what they can and cannot do—in order to push the boundaries of technology. Only those who know the existing rules of computers can create the hardware, software, and programming languages of tomorrow and, by extension, the new forms of thought and expression.

On a spiritual level, "Enter by form, exit from form" says we enter this world by form through our material bodies, and exit from those bodies when we die—we transcend the form. It is no different on the computer. We "enter by form" by logging on to the machine. The tool becomes an extension of our mind and body. We "exit from form" through use of the tool. The tool becomes a means to an end—a vehicle through which our spirit passes as we produce work.

The next time you hit ENTER, ask yourself: What am I entering? Is it a command? A piece of data? Or can it be the gates of enlightenment?

Option/Alternate

All err the more dangerously because each follows a truth. Their mistake lies not in following a falsehood but in not following another truth.

—BLAISE PASCAL (1623–62),
FRENCH SCIENTIST, MATHEMATICIAN, PHILOSOPHER

Some computers come equipped with an OPTION key; others call it ALTERNATE. The basic idea is the same: Whether on the computer or off, we always have an option or alternative—a key that gives us choice. Sometimes we don't realize it but, on a fundamental level, we hold the option to pursue the path of self-cultivation; to see the glass as half empty or half full; to affirm life, even with all its sorrow and pain.

We can act with compassion, seek the help of others, put our children first—do everything we know to be right and true.

The option is there at every moment—and it's ours to choose. Let the OPTION/ALTERNATE key be your reminder.

Command/Control

*What I've enjoyed from the beginning is that with
programming there's . . . a very direct line between
having an idea and making it happen. It's just you versus
yourself: you ask yourself, can you focus, can you create
a good design, can you implement it?*

—MICHAEL BUDIANSKY, FOUNDER, QUADRIVIO CORP.

L ike the SHIFT and OPTION/ALTERNATE keys, COMMAND
and CONTROL are modifier keys. Pressed by themselves,
they effect no change. Only when pressed in conjunction with
a mouse click or another key do they modify the action.

We should think of command and control in life the same
way. To pursue command and control for their own sake is an
empty goal; such pursuit amounts to nothing more than lust
for power. But when we combine command and control with
self-cultivation, we begin to modify our actions in a meaningful way.

Try as you might to command others, some will not listen.
Command yourself, though, and you will always do your own
bidding. To demonstrate such self-command is to demonstrate
mastery.

Try as you might to control the events and people around
you, you will reach your limits—be you king, queen, or com-

moner. But the path of self-control has no end. Follow it, and no one will ever own you.

Escape

Every person has free choice. Free to obey or disobey the Natural Laws. Your choice determines the consequences. Nobody ever did, or ever will, escape the consequences of his choices.

—Alfred A. Montapert, author,
Supreme Philosophy of Man

The ESCAPE key offers a way out of a computer function we don't want to continue. Sometimes, though, it doesn't work—the function continues no matter how many times we hit the key. Such is life. Try as we might to escape a problem, we cannot avoid it forever. We can travel the world to hide if something bothers us, but wherever we go, there we are—we carry our problem with us. Sometimes the only way out of personal torment is to realize there is no escape, and stare the demon down.

Remember, the demon is not out there. It lives within. If the ESCAPE key doesn't work, don't blame the machine. Deal with the problem inside.

Tab

If I had to sum up in one word what makes a good manager, I'd say decisiveness. You can use the fanciest computers to gather the numbers, but in the end you have to set a timetable and act.

—Lee Iacocca,
former chairman, Chrysler Corp.

The TAB key advances the cursor to the next stopping point. We should all move so quickly upon making a decision. Even though the way of zen is to slow down and live calmly, there is a difference between rushing around and moving decisively.

To rush around is to act out of haste, to feel pressed for time. To move decisively is to move quickly, under control, with no feeling of haste.

In waiting at a stop sign to turn left into traffic, we sometimes get antsy and proceed before we should. Other times we hesitate for a moment and miss our chance to move. When mind and body are coordinated, thought and action occur simultaneously. We wait calmly until the precise moment, then hit the gas and seamlessly join the flow of traffic. All action should be like this. The instant we think to move, we hit the TAB key and go—not hurried, not hesitating. Just decisive and efficient.

At the point of rest, we rest.

Space Bar

Not everything that can be counted counts, and not everything that counts can be counted.

—Albert Einstein (1879–1955)

The SPACE BAR is the biggest key on the keyboard, and for good reason. No key is more important. Where all the other keys leave a mark, the space bar leaves the absence of a mark. This absence gives the marks meaning and rhythm.

Musicians have a saying, "Music is the space between the notes." The same is true on a page. Space creates form, form creates space. Together, they express the interplay of yin and yang. What gives each letter its shape? Space. What gives letters strung together any meaning? Space.

We often like to measure our progress in life with markers—birthdays, anniversaries, graduation days, retirement. Let the space bar represent all those moments in between, when the cursor moves forward without leaving a mark. There, too, we're making progress.

Where there is no space, there is only the void.

Delete

*Perfection is achieved, not when there is nothing left to add,
but when there is nothing left to take away.*

—ANTOINE DE SAINT-EXUPÉRY, AUTHOR,
THE LITTLE PRINCE

The DELETE key, known on some machines as the BACK SPACE key, erases typos and mistakes and anything else we want to clear. After the space bar, no key gets more use. Yet we still don't use DELETE enough. We leave far too much on the page.

As a rule, nothing should appear on a page unless it is essential. If it's not essential, delete it. This is the zen aesthetic—nothing extra. When a composer writes a symphony, every note should belong. When a poet writes a poem, every word and punctuation mark should belong. When programmers write their code, every line should matter. Resist the temptation to show off—to add bells and whistles simply because you can. If one line of code will suffice instead of three, delete the other two. If you find a single element superfluous, why keep it there? When in doubt, leave it out.

Do not underestimate the rigor required in such thinking. To pare something down to its essentials takes hard work and clarity of mind. As Blaise Pascal once said to a friend, "I have made this letter longer than usual, only because I have not had time to make it shorter." It's much easier to blather than focus our thoughts in an elegant way. Think of all the documents produced in this world. How many could have been strengthened by being pared in half? How many were necessary to produce at all?

The same rules apply to life. We carry so much baggage around with us, materially and emotionally. Our closets are stuffed with clothes we don't wear; our minds are cluttered with thinking that gets us nowhere. We need to hit the DELETE key more often.

A writing teacher of mine said she could always tell when a student had fallen in love with a fancy turn of phrase for its own sake. It would stick out in the story and sound nice, but never quite fit with the flow of the work. "Much as it kills you," she would say, "you have to cut those little darlings out."

In life, art, or the computer: To use the DELETE key properly, you have to be ruthless. Leave only what's essential.

Less is more.

Return

it your RETURN key.

Leave the previous line behind.

Proceed anew, with a beginner's mind.

▽ 📁 Hardware
   ▽ 📁 Mouse
      📄 *Point*
      📄 *Click*
      📄 *Drag & Drop*

Mouse

You can use the mouse with either hand.

—MACINTOSH USER'S GUIDE,
"HOW TO HOLD THE MOUSE"

A long with the keyboard, the mouse is our other area of contact with the machine, and the same lessons of mind-body coordination apply. With the keyboard, the mind directs the fingers over a complex field of keys. The mouse, on the other hand, moves in any direction along the plane of the screen. This puts a greater emphasis on eye-to-hand coordination—the hand moves the mouse to where the eye goes.

Through practice, we come to see the coordination of eye and hand as the integration of the senses—sight and touch acting in concert. We realize that all the senses—sight, sound, taste, touch, and smell—are not five separate things so much as one complete thing. In fact, all components of the body—from head and shoulders, knees and toes, to eyes and ears and mouth and nose—are one thing.

Too often we put our minds in one part of the body, or allow one of our senses (usually sight) to dominate our experience. The result is a disconnection between the body's constituent parts. To coordinate mind and body means three things:

1. **The mind is coordinated with the body.** As the mind directs the body, so the body responds.

2. **The mind is coordinated with itself.** Thoughts are focused, not scattered.

3. **The body is coordinated with itself.** The parts of the body work in unison, not awkwardly or independently.

Coordination of mind and body requires a coordination with spirit as well. For without the proper spirit, we cannot endeavor to focus the mind or train the body. These endeavors demand an exertion of will.

The zen master Takuan advises to "put the mind no place." If, through hard training and meditation, we can achieve that difficult state, the mind, like the mouse, will be free to move as we please.

A few reminders of mindful thinking, focusing on use of the mouse, follow.

Point

I see your point . . . and raise you a line.

—Elliot Smorodinsky, system administrator,
Eclipse America Corp.

Zen teaching is said to be like a finger pointing to the moon. Do not concentrate on the finger, zen masters say, or you'll miss the moon in all its heavenly glory. In other words, zen is only a guide to the truth. It is not the truth itself.

Let the arrow on your computer screen remind you of a finger pointing to the moon. With the proper frame of mind, all things become a guide to the truth, from a flower to a rock to a computer screen. The truth assumes infinite shapes and forms. The challenge is to realize the truth wherever you look.

Note, too, that wherever you move the mouse, the arrow always points in the same direction. It may point at this item or that icon, a file over here or a folder over there, but it always points upward. That is to say, the way to the truth never varies. No matter what our culture or religious beliefs, no matter what our understanding of zen, we all know the way to the truth lies in honesty, integrity, self-discipline, faith, and love. If only it were as simple a path to follow as to say.

Keep the arrow in your eye and follow it, onward and upward.

Click

Eureka! Eureka!

—ARCHIMEDES (287–212 B.C.), ON DISCOVERING A METHOD
FOR DETERMINING THE PURITY OF GOLD

E ach click of the mouse represents a distinct moment in time. As fast as we can doubleclick, two distinct moments go by. How brief the moment. How swift the passage of time.

Zen masters say that every moment offers the chance for enlightenment. Our true nature, they say, can be known in an instant, if only we're of the mind to realize it.

Take a moment and listen to the click of your mouse. There, in that single sound, lies an opportunity—for *hearing* what you're doing; for connecting mind and body, thought and action, user and machine; for being completely present in the moment.

Meditate long enough and, with a single click of the mouse, you will hear the sound of the truth.

Drag & Drop

A file that big?
It might be very useful.
But now it is gone.

—COMPUTER HAIKU POSTED
ON THE INTERNET

With the drag-and-drop feature, we select something on the screen to pick up, drag to another place, and drop at a new destination. This feature brings to mind a parable about the zen master Tanzan and his disciple Ekido.

On a rainy day, the two men came upon a woman looking to cross a muddy road in her silk kimono. "Allow me," said Tanzan. He lifted the woman in his arms and carried her across the divide.

Later on that evening, Ekido approached his master. "As monks, we've taken strict ascetic vows," he said. "We're not supposed to touch the opposite sex. How could you pick that woman up?"

"I put the woman down at the side of the road," Tanzan said. "Are you still carrying her?"

Let the drag-and-drop feature remind us of Tanzan's lesson. When we pick something up, we pick it up mindfully, naturally, without regard to strictures and rules. When we put it down, we let it go and move on.

We cling to so many things, refusing to let go—a relationship that's over, an age that's passed us by, an image of ourselves that's distorted, a safe little station in life that keeps us from growing. We've dragged these things with us far enough. In life, as on the computer: Drop it and move on.

Hard Drive

E very machine has its moving parts. For the computer, it's the hard drive, also known as the hard disk. For those people unfamiliar with computers, the hard drive is a stack of round, magnetic platters inside a case connected to the motherboard. They act as the computer's main storage system. Like a tape recorder, they play back (read) and record (write) all the information that gets stored on your computer. When a computer is running, the constant whirring sound you hear is the fans cooling, among other things, those platters spinning around furiously, handling gigantic amounts of data.

The hard drive reminds us of where the heavy work gets done in this world—the engine rooms, back offices, printing presses, and blast furnaces. For every person in this economy gazing at a computer screen, there's someone behind the scenes doing the heavy lifting, mining the coal, tilling the soil, moving the merchandise.

Be mindful of these workhorses when you hear that hard drive whirring. Like the blockers who clear the way for the ball carrier to score, they get little recognition. Yet nothing gets done without them.

Out of sight, maybe, but not out of mind.

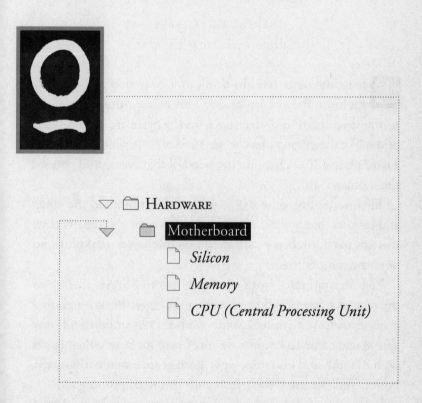

▽ 📂 HARDWARE
    ▽ 📂 Motherboard
        📄 *Silicon*
        📄 *Memory*
        📄 *CPU (Central Processing Unit)*

Motherboard

Any sufficiently advanced technology
is indistinguishable from magic.

—ARTHUR C. CLARKE,
SCIENCE-FICTION WRITER

irst-time users tend to think of a computer as being the monitor and the keyboard. This is like thinking of a car as the dashboard and steering wheel. The heart of the computer, like the engine of a car, sits hidden from view, encased in a hard plastic box. Open up the hood of that casing and you see the motherboard.

The motherboard holds the guts of the computer, the chips and circuits that make it run. Just as a car engine has many constituent parts, such as a carburetor, oil filter, and sparkplugs, so does the motherboard.

Like all mothers—from Mother Earth to Mother Nature to the mother of every child and every one of us—the motherboard gives birth to something magic. We need not understand how this magic came to be, but we must care for it responsibly. As with Aladdin and his lamp, we've been given a tremendous new power. Will we use it for selfish ends or the common good?

Remember, from one mother, new mothers are born. As the motherboard of your computer brings into this world a unique capability, so should you, in turn through your work, give birth to a new creation. Put your heart and soul into that creation. Nurture and care for it, in sacrifice to future generations. Raise it up so that it may honor the Great Mother of us all.

Silicon

An educated mind is, as it were, composed of all the minds of preceding ages.

—Bernard Le Bovier Fontenelle (1657–1757),
mathematical historian

Silicon is the most common material used to make computer chips, the tiny building blocks of computers strung together on the motherboard that produce the magic on every screen. So central is the material's role in technology that when the region south of San Francisco emerged as the world's epicenter of computer entrepreneurship, pundits named it Silicon Valley.

Silicon's chemical properties perfectly suit a computer chip's need to hold millions of electronic components and circuits. Plus, the material is cheap and widely available. Silicon is one of the most abundant chemical elements on the planet, found in sand and clay. In essence, the computer industry has arisen from the very sands of the earth.

From the merest of beginnings, we, too, arise on this earth, grow, and make our way. And to the earth we one day return. In between, we can only help those coming after us to stand on our shoulders.

So it was for Baron Jons Jakob Berzelius. So it may be for you.

Who was Berzelius?

He discovered silicon back in 1823.

How high will those who follow you go?

Memory

Out of memory.
We wish to hold the whole sky,
But we never will.

—COMPUTER HAIKU POSTED ON THE INTERNET

A particular kind of computer chip on the motherboard is the memory chip. The function of the memory chip is to remember what we've instructed the machine to do, and what we ourselves have done.

We ask the computer to remember things both short term and long term. In the short term, computer memory stores what we need to keep available for random access—things we're working on right now, that we need to retrieve quickly. Techies call it *random-access memory* (RAM). Regardless of how much RAM we have, it always seems we'd like to have more. The same goes for our human short-term memory—especially at those times we can't remember where we set our keys down or if we turned off the stove.

Short-term memory is a measure of mindfulness. If we're truly paying attention to what we're doing, we cannot help but remember where we put things or what we just did.

Long-term memory is another story. So many things work their way into our long-term memories, who can say how they get there? The sound of a distant foghorn, the smell of cookies baking in the oven, the scrap of paper we come across while cleaning the closet—the merest signal can trigger a vibrant memory.

Sometimes we're surprised at what the computer remembers, too. We forget that all the records of life are stored now on some machine, on disk or tape or something else. With just a few bits of data, people can put together a highly personal dossier on us: our phone calls, credit card use, bank accounts, tax returns, medical records, school grades, employment history, legal entanglements, criminal past—all the specifics of our lives on paper. Some people are more than willing to take these facts and twist them for their own purposes, unconcerned with knowing the truth.

Certain memories can haunt us and fill our lives with regret if we fail to come to terms with them. We cannot change what we have done; we can only move forward, mindful of what we've done and what we're now doing. In zen, each moment presents an opportunity to create new memories—the kind that can enrich our lives and define anew who we are.

In Fyodor Dostoyevsky's *The Brothers Karamazov,* the priest Alyosha urges a group of boys to create these kinds of vital memories, the ones that can inform a person's whole life:

> You must know that there is nothing higher and stronger and more wholesome and good for life in the future than some good memory, especially a memory of childhood, of home. People talk to you a great deal about your education, but some good sacred memory, preserved from childhood, is the best education. If a man carries many such memories with him into life, he is safe to the end of his days.

Build strong memories, the kind that will shape and educate the generations to follow. As survivors of the Holocaust and atomic bombs know, some memories need to be passed on forever.

However, do not live in the past. Too many people live lost in memory of days gone by. Zen demands that we never stop living for today. Even in the twilight of our years, do any of us want a life where the days slide right through our hands, where nothing happens that's worth remembering?

Let the computer remember the prose of life—the mundane details devoid of flesh and blood. Fill your own memory with the poetry.

CPU (Central Processing Unit)

Few, but ripe.

—MOTTO OF CARL FRIEDRICH GAUSS (1777–1855),
GERMAN MATHEMATICIAN, PHYSICIST, AND ASTRONOMER

nother unique computer chip on the motherboard is called the central processing unit, or CPU. The CPU serves as the computer's brains, the area where all the 1s and 0s of information get processed and translated.

We rate our CPUs according to speed and efficiency, the faster the better. We tend to want the same from our brains. When the pressure's on, we tell ourselves, *think faster.*

The way to zen, though, is not through thinking faster. Do without thinking, zen masters say. Move in the way the ripe fruit falls from the tree—naturally, when the time is right. Zen is the point where thought and action are simultaneous.

So often we hesitate in life, trying to compute the risk/reward ratio and play the percentages. We take polls, do focus groups, hire consultants to buttress our decision-making. Zen says follow your intuition. There are times when calculations only confuse.

A computer can calculate so many chess moves a second that even the world champion can't beat it, yet it still can't lead a child across a busy street. Life requires a *sense* of things. Do not underestimate the importance of intuition.

The same goes for imagination. We can have the fastest computer in the world, but what good is that speed if we fail to see its new possibilities, if we lack the vision to bring it the right problems, if all the new machine bears is the pedestrian, the mundane, the usual? There is a difference between driving a sports car fast simply because we can and driving it to get somewhere.

So many of us complain that the world of computers is speeding up our lives. But we can go nowhere faster.

Repeat: *We can go nowhere faster.*

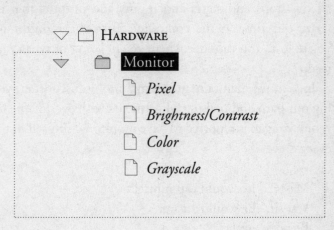

▽ 🗀 HARDWARE

　　▽ 🗀 Monitor

　　　🗋 *Pixel*

　　　🗋 *Brightness/Contrast*

　　　🗋 *Color*

　　　🗋 *Grayscale*

Monitor

Serious error.
All shortcuts have disappeared.
Screen. Mind. Both blank.

—Computer haiku posted on the Internet

The computer monitor shows us the state of our work *right now.* Each moment is an update of the last, reflecting all the stops and starts and inputs and outputs that characterize our time at the computer. Turn the monitor off and you're lost. You can't see where you're going or what you need to do.

In zen, we maintain an internal monitor, constantly checking our path and making adjustments with every step. The zen monk Zuigan is reported to have monitored himself in this way every day.

"Master," he would call himself.
"Yes, sir," he would answer.
"Be wide awake!"
"Yes, sir."
"And don't be deceived by others."
"No, I won't."

Zuigan knew that the mind hears many conflicting voices and can easily be led astray. His lesson is that we need to continually monitor ourselves—minding mind—if we're to stay focused on the moment and keep our thoughts on track.

Turn off the monitor and it's easy to lose the way.

Pixel

Through space the universe grasps me and swallows me up like a speck; through thought I grasp it.

—BLAISE PASCAL (1623–62)

The fundamental unit on computer screens is the pixel, short for picture element. Each pixel is a tiny dot of light, whose character is controlled by data on the computer. Together, hundreds of thousands of pixels combine to form the image you see on the screen.

Pixels remind us that all things in this universe consist of the tiniest elements. Even a single grain of sand is made of millions of atoms. That grain of sand looks like a speck against the expanse of the cosmos—completely insignificant. Yet the infinitely big is born of the infinitely small. That speck is there: It cannot be otherwise.

When we think of all the pixels on our screen, how vast the

world of a single computer looks. Then we look to the heavens and see the stars. How small our problems, our quarrels, our silly egos.

Through zen we put ourselves in the middle, perceiving both truths at once. Up close, we care about the placement of every pixel in our work, knowing the path to self-betterment lies in attention to the smallest details. At the same time we remain humbled by the scale of all that surrounds us. We live knowing that we are only one among the many, and yet we *are*.

It cannot be otherwise.

Brightness/Contrast

The structures with which mathematics deals are more like . . . the play of the light and shadow on a human face than they are like buildings and machines, the least of their representatives.

—SCOTT BUCHANAN, AUTHOR,
POETRY AND MATHEMATICS

When adjusting the brightness and contrast on our computer screens, we find the balance of yin and yang. No need for statistical measures, just sensing that place that's not too dark and not too bright—right between the two.

Now extend that eye toward everything around you. There you have it:

Zen.

Color

I believe in . . . the mystery of color.

—GEORGE BERNARD SHAW (1856–1950)

E very color that appears on your computer screen can be broken down mathematically into its component parts, as percentages of red, green, and blue light (RGB). Incredibly, a whole universe of color arises just through various combinations of RGB.

But, as anyone who's worked with color can tell you, what you see on the screen is not what you get on the printed page. The same red that looks so good on your computer screen can look a lot different when printed in ink.

The printing process divides the world of color into four parts instead of three: cyan, magenta, yellow, and black (CMYK). Thus, transferring colors from computer screen to print requires experience and follow-through.

We can spend hours perfecting an image on our computer screen, getting it to look exactly as we would like, but we sometimes forget that the job isn't done until the printed output looks good. Through trial and error or the advice of an expert, we learn how to prepare the colors on our computer so the output begins to match our vision. The process may take repeated tweaking and adjustments, but we stay on it until it's done right.

Zen lies in the attitude of following through. On the screen, the colors may look perfect, but you always have to keep going, doing color correction, maintaining quality. Finish this job, move on to the next. To stop in satisfaction at any point is to lose the thread of zen.

Carry on, follow through, ever closer to that place where all the colors bleed into one.

Grayscale

I call this the mismatch problem: The world is gray
but science is black and white. We talk in zeroes and
ones but the truth lies in between.

—BART KOSKO, AUTHOR, *FUZZY THINKING*

When working in black and white, grayscale refers to all the gray tones available between absolute black and absolute white. Most computer monitors can render 256 shades of gray. In zen, the levels are infinite.

Within the interlocking fetal figures that comprise the yin-yang symbol, the black side contains a small circle of white and the white side contains a small circle of black. So the moment something in the mind becomes absolutely black or absolutely white, zen disappears. In any given situation, zen says, there is always a larger picture to consider, and a smaller one, too—circles within you and without you.

For some people, this thinking challenges the notion of ethical standards. If we apply yin-yang to morality, can we truly say that anything is right or wrong? The answer is yes and no.

All of us have a personal compass telling us what's right and wrong. Humanity *should* stand united against the abusers of the world, the rapists, the child molesters, the warmongers and tyrants. However, we can no more eradicate the darkest impulses of human nature than we can stop the earthquakes that bury villages or the hurricanes that level seaside towns. All are manifestations of nature, and though we may battle against them, on some level we must also learn how to live with them in our midst. Without evil, there is no good; without ugliness, there is no beauty. Each defines the other as two sides of the human coin.

In addition, we all know there's a huge gray area between right and wrong. As is often said, one person's terrorist is another person's freedom fighter. In such cases, who determines what is evil? The challenge for any society is to navigate the gray area between security and personal freedom, the will of the majority and the rights of the minority. Go too far in one direction and you disrupt the delicate balance of yin and yang.

So, we wage our battles according to our beliefs, fighting for the black within the larger white truth and the white within the black, all part of the great gray dance of nature. The only absolute compass to follow is zen.

Seeking that compass, a student once asked a zen master, "What is the solution that accounts for every situation?"

The master replied, "As the situation arises."

Understand that, and you can look upon the grayscale of your computer and see the one brilliant color.

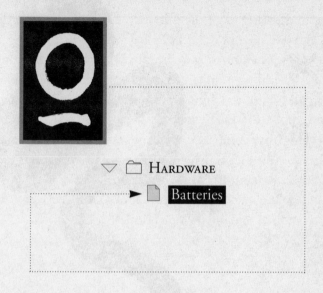

▽ 📁 Hᴀʀᴅᴡᴀʀᴇ
► 📄 Batteries

Batteries

L ike battery, like body:

Energy flows through, giving vibrance to all it touches.

Battery dies, body dies: All things must pass.

New battery, new body.

Same energy.

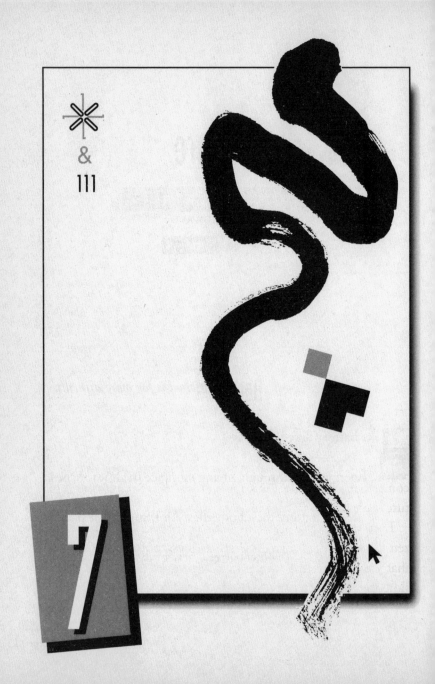

7

Software

There are two ways of constructing a software design: One way is to make it so simple that there are no obvious deficiencies, and the other way is to make it so complicated that there are no obvious deficiencies. The first method is far more difficult.
—C. A. R. HOARE, PROFESSOR OF COMPUTING, OXFORD UNIVERSITY

SOFTWARE CONSISTS OF the coded instructions that tell a computer what to do. As stated earlier, software's formless nature serves as yin to the yang of hardware.

Even though yin and yang are forever entwined, the way of zen identifies with softness over hardness. Softness is the water that wears down the stone, the compassion that greets aggression, the womb that envelopes the form. Where hardware's output is fixed by physical limitations, software's is open to the imagination of the user.

The characteristics of softness—flexibility, easiness, fluidity—are to be prized in software and, by extension, the mind. After all, the coded instructions of software spring directly from the clarity and complexity of our thoughts. The more these thoughts flow, the more the software flows.

Recognize, though, that within the yin, there is always a bit of yang. The moment one's thoughts become hard and rigid, software begins to lose its possibilities.

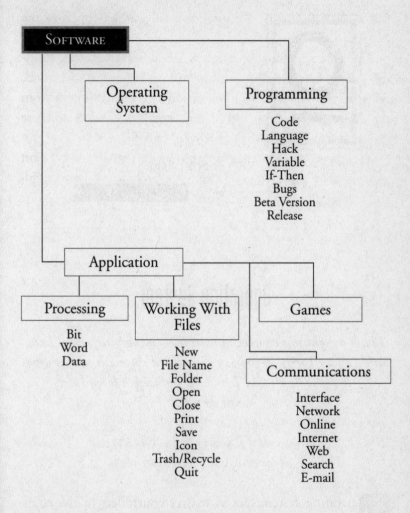

SOFTWARE

Operating System

Programming

Code
Language
Hack
Variable
If-Then
Bugs
Beta Version
Release

Application

Processing

Bit
Word
Data

Working With Files

New
File Name
Folder
Open
Close
Print
Save
Icon
Trash/Recycle
Quit

Games

Communications

Interface
Network
Online
Internet
Web
Search
E-mail

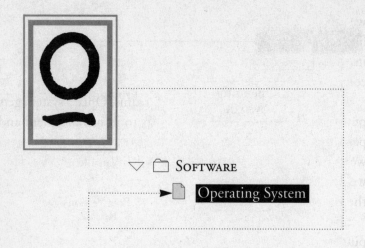

▽ 🗀 SOFTWARE

▶ 🗋 Operating System

Operating System

I have bought this wonderful machine—a computer. Now I am rather an authority on gods, so I identified the machine—it seems to me to be an Old Testament god with a lot of rules and no mercy.

—JOSEPH CAMPBELL (1904–87),
MYTHOLOGY SCHOLAR

perating systems act as master controllers of the computer, dictating what we can do on the machine and how we can do it. In some ways, the different operating systems are like competing religions. Each has its own rules and symbols, its passionate adherents and leaders bent on gaining new converts.

We create these systems to serve our aims. Once a system gets put in place, however, our focus shifts to its advancement and perpetuation. We become forced to work within the system we've built; its limitations become our limitations. The more we get locked into a system, the more we become servants of the very thing crafted to serve us.

Sometimes a religion can suffocate people of faith if it starts putting the commands of the church above the spiritual life of its flock. It forgets that the church should be a means for people to *transcend* the church, that religion should be the vehicle of religious experience.

If we feel stifled by a system, we cannot tear it down without replacing it with something else. And while the replacement may be better or worse, like all systems, it will still grow out of human concepts and thus have limitations.

That which Zen Computer seeks lies beyond the realm of concepts and limitations. The only way we get there is to transcend the system. Use the system to rise above it. All things have a mystical element that speaks to the presence of something divine. You need not look for it somewhere else— it's there in your system right now. See it through Zen Computer.

▽ 🗀 SOFTWARE
　　▽ 🗀 Programming
　　　　🖹 *Code*
　　　　🖹 *Language*
　　　　🖹 *Hack*
　　　　🖹 *Variable*
　　　　🖹 *If-Then*
　　　　🖹 *Bugs*
　　　　🖹 *Beta Version*
　　　　🖹 *Release*

Programming

The computer programmer is a creator of universes
for which he alone is responsible.

—Joseph Weizenbaum,
MIT professor of computer science,
author, *Computer Power and Human Reason*

A computer without instructions is just an expensive doorstop—a heap of plastic, wire, and metal. Programming tells the computer what to do.

This raises a couple of fundamental questions: What do we want the machine to do and how do we want the machine to do it?

It may seem obvious to ask ourselves the basic purpose of writing a program, but so often we muddle the answer. The computing world abounds with clunky, inefficient, even useless software, the result of programmers who failed to think clearly about what they were doing and why. It may not matter so much when we're writing programs for ourselves—so long as it works, we're happy—but writing programs for other people requires a higher standard of care.

The essential function of programming should be to help users do what they want to do, go where they want to go, and know what they want to know as quickly, easily, and efficiently as possible. Too often we forget that. We don't take the time to figure out precisely what the user wants, or think through the best way it can be done. If we're on a team of programmers, we may lack a strong leader with a strong vision, or there may be collaborators who aren't working toward a common goal. Maybe they're more interested in showing off their skill as programmers, throwing in bells and whistles the user doesn't need, simply because they can.

The zen way to think of programming would be to follow the spirit of the Japanese tea ceremony, or *Chado,* the Way of Tea. In Chado, the ritual act of a host serving tea and a guest gratefully receiving it serves as a model for all human relations. The host welcomes the guest; the guest extends sincere appreciation for the hospitality. Through sharing a bowl of tea, host and guest commune as one and, in that small way, seek to harmonize the discord of the world.

Japan's most famous tea master, Sen Rikyu, was once asked by a disciple, "What are the most important things to keep in mind during a tea gathering?"

Rikyu replied,

Make a delicious bowl of tea;
Lay the charcoal so that it heats the water;
Arrange the flowers as they are in the field;
In summer suggest coolness, in winter, warmth;
Do everything ahead of time;

Prepare for rain;
Give those with whom you find yourself every consideration.

"That much I already know," the disciple said.

To which Rikyu said, "If you can host a tea gathering without deviating from any of the rules I have just stated, I will become your disciple."

THE SEVEN RULES OF RIKYU have since been handed down through the generations as the essence of Chado, but they stand as a model for anyone in the business of providing service, including programmers. Because, in the end, all programming should boil down to three words: Serve the user.

Let's consider Rikyu's rules in the context of programming.

1. Make a delicious bowl of tea. When endeavoring to write a program, write the best, most elegant program possible, and do so *on behalf of the user.* Use the finest ingredients available, but more than that, put your heart into it. Tea masters call this *kokoro ire*—"inclusion of the heart's spirit." Serve the user not because you have to, but because you want to.

Kokoro ire

2. Lay the charcoal so that it heats the water. This seems obvious, but Rikyu's point speaks to efficiency and the use of resources. Don't use too much charcoal or it will go to waste; don't use too little charcoal or it won't generate the needed heat. Write a program that serves its purpose. Avoid the unnecessary additions that slow a program down, but make sure it doesn't lack what the user needs.

3. Arrange the flowers as they are in the field. Every tea ceremony has as its visual focal point a modest, fresh-cut flower arrangement. These flowers are not simply strewn about "as they are in the field," but rather aesthetically placed so as to heighten their natural beauty.

Any human arrangement reveals something about the way our mind works. Rikyu reminds us that our inner sense of order should align itself with the natural order. Whatever program we write should feel natural and intuitive to the user. How many times when working with a user-friendly program do we know it can perform certain functions, even before looking at the manual? "Of *course* it can do this," we say, because it's natural to the way the program feels. There is no showy display of programming skill. Just the opposite—the skill of the programmer isn't even noticed.

4. In summer suggest coolness, in winter, warmth. The ritual of a tea ceremony starts long before the host pours the first cup of tea or the guests arrive. Great consideration goes into making the surroundings comfortable, spraying water on the sunbeaten walkway to cool it off in summer, placing lanterns in winter to give the room a warm glow.

In computer terms, this rule applies to the so-called operating environment. Think to write a program that's inviting the moment a user boots it up. It should be easy on the eyes and well laid out. It should have a familiar feeling even to those who've never seen the program before. Every detail on the screen presents an opportunity to show you've thought about the user's needs.

5. Do everything ahead of time. No host wants to run around after the guests have arrived, still making preparations. Likewise, it should be common sense for programmers to check their software before it's sent to users. Too often, software gets released to the public with programmers still scrambling to fix it. Test and retest ahead of time.

Admittedly, the complex architecture of some software may make it impossible to fully debug. Also, market pressures may necessitate a hasty release, but there is an honest effort that too many companies simply fail to make. That failure leads to many more frustrated users than necessary, and much more time spent responding to customer complaints. Both have their costs.

Do your customer service *ahead of time.* Then, when the user comes to your program, you can both sit back and enjoy.

6. Prepare for rain. Unforeseen things can happen. A new program might be incompatible with an existing one, causing problems. The operating system you've written your program for might get radically overhauled. The user might become confused and inadvertently change a key setting within the program, rendering it unworkable.

We can't prepare for every possible eventuality. But for some things, like rain, we can. Anticipate those and take care to deal with them by building a strong technical support system. As the tea masters say, "With preparation there is no regret."

7. Give those with whom you find yourself every consideration. This rule might be called the Way of User-Friendliness. It's not enough to write a user-friendly program. Every aspect of the user's experience with the computer should feel welcoming. The packaging should look inviting. The price should be right. The documentation should be easy to read and understand. The installation process should be smooth. The application should run clean and make intuitive sense. Customer service should be patient, friendly, and helpful. Upgrades should improve performance and add only necessary features. These things can only result from a culture of user-friendliness— one in which every consideration is given to the user.

BY FOLLOWING RIKYU'S RULES, we develop the quality of empathy, learning to put ourselves in the mind of the user. Because, ultimately, all programmers are users as well; there is no divide. The tools and languages that define the programmer's trade have all been developed by a line of engineers who've come before and given of themselves to *their* users, the programmers.

Therein lies the circle that makes the tea ceremony a model for human relations: uniting the mind of host and guest. As the host learns to empathize with the guest, the guest learns to empathize with the host. If programmers give every consideration to the user, the user will reciprocate with gratitude—ask any of the thousands of programmers who offer their work freely over the Internet and experience the genuine thanks of strangers. The challenge becomes one of extending Chado's attitude of friendliness to all relations, away from the tea ceremony, away from computer, into the world at large.

The Way of User-Friendliness arises from within. Cultivate it and carry it with you always.

Code

In the idiom of the moment, let us propound the ultimate law of God in the information age: In the beginning was the word—the code—and it is not reducible to anything else.

—George Gilder,
senior fellow, the Discover Institute

A computer can only do what is written in its code. Once written, the code rules the machine like a dictator. It tells the machine what to do and how to do it in the exact manner. If we want the machine to do something differently, we have to change the code it is running.

As human beings, we, too, have a fixed internal code. Our genetic code determines much about who we are and what we become. The day will arrive when we can alter that code and change the very formula of human life.

Those who control the code, whether on the machine level or the human level, hold tremendous power. Power demands the wisdom and humility to use it responsibly. As a society, we must work to ensure that a higher code guides our actions—our moral code.

Instead of trying to *play* God by controlling a piece of code, let the God-spirit inherent in all things manifest itself through you. If you endeavor to know the ultimate source code first, no other code will matter.

Language

The union of the mathematician with the poet, fervor with measure, passion with correctness, this surely is the ideal.

—WILLIAM JAMES (1842–1910)

Programmers write their code using various computer languages such as HTML, Java, and C++. Each has its own strengths and weaknesses. Ultimately, the language that programmers use depends on what they want to communicate; in the same way that a Japanese word might convey a feeling better than its English counterpart, so do some computer languages express an idea more precisely than others.

Some people use the language so well they achieve the level of poetry. There are programs of such clarity and power they evoke feelings of aesthetic beauty, like a computer science haiku. The architecture of thought is so pure one senses a higher truth at work. Programmers call it a feeling of "elegance."

Of course, the average user may know nothing of elegant code. In the same way it took fellow painters to first understand the achievement of a Cézanne, it often takes fellow programmers to see the depth of an elegant program. Who knows the difficulty of the achievement better than another who has tried to achieve it?

We all have our private view into excellence, whatever our

walk of life—unsung heroes whose names are known only to us, whose achievement goes unrecognized by all except those people close enough to notice. Maybe it's the systems manager at work who solved the office network problem, maybe it's the librarian who knows just the right way to search a database, or maybe it's simply a parent who raised a family through trying times. The examples abound around us. So much of what seems routine in life is in fact elegant and extraordinary, if we just know how to see it.

Let those examples inspire us to find our own elegance, in anything we do: to see clearly, speak clearly, say the most with the least. Infuse *every* expression with a sense of poetry—every word, every sound, every movement—for those are the small steps that help us climb the spiritual mountain and give others a glimpse through the clouds. Whatever the language, be it Java or Japanese, the rule is the same.

Call it elegance, call it excellence, call it poetry.

Call it zen.

Hack

Hacking might be characterized as "an appropriate application of ingenuity." Whether the result is a quick-and-dirty patchwork job or a carefully crafted work of art, you have to admire the cleverness that went into it.

—THE JARGON FILE, "THE MEANING OF HACK"

ack is a slang term that can mean a relentless approach to computer use, the technological equivalent of taking a machete to thick brush. It sometimes refers to the hardcore, often trial-and-error method of computer enthusiasts who acquire vast technical knowledge without formal training.

Through misuse, the term hack has become synonymous with illegal activity, such as breaking into a computer system and stealing data, but its original meaning is benign.

Whatever the ends, hacking requires sheer determination, a mindset that refuses to take no for an answer. To hack is to pursue an end until every obstacle is overcome.

Zen requires a similar approach. At zen monasteries in Japan, prospective monks are put to the test from the start. Anyone who comes seeking admittance to the monastery is immediately rejected and told to leave. The most determined refuse to go. They sit for hours at the entryway, heads bowed, silently seeking acceptance. Eventually, they are forcibly removed from the vestibule. Those still more determined return, resuming their impassive pose, sometimes for days with no food or drink. Only after they've demonstrated that level of fortitude are they accepted for training.

Remember, though, that even the attitude of relentless pursuit requires balance. If hacking should turn into obsessive computer use, the user has strayed far from the path of zen. The more we seek a highly focused goal or pursue a narrow field of knowledge, the more we need to see it from the broadest possible outlook.

Hack away relentlessly at the thick brush in front of you. But do so seeing the forest for the trees.

Variable

One person's constant is another person's variable.

—SUSAN GERHART, RESEARCH INSTITUTE
FOR COMPUTING AND INFORMATION SYSTEMS, UNIVERSITY
OF HOUSTON AT CLEAR LAKE

A variable is a symbol in computer programming that can assume a value later. In the expression X + Y, for example, X and Y are variables. These variables give a program flexibility, enabling it to work with different sets of data. The first time through a program, the variable X can stand for one thing; the next time through, it can stand for something else.

Zen allows for innumerable variables. Its truths can be known through anything—a river, a caterpillar, a pebble, a computer. Every action and every moment offers an opportunity to experience the same great truth.

A monk once approached the zen master Kempo and said, "It is written, 'All Buddhas enter the one straight road to Nirvana [unity with the absolute].' I still wonder where that road can be."

Kempo drew a line in the air with his staff and said: "Here it is."

To find the truth of zen, use whatever variable you wish. Any one can work.

X marks the spot.

If-Then

I never think of the future—it comes soon enough.

—ALBERT EINSTEIN (1879–1955)

One of the common expressions in computer programming is the if-then statement: "If A = B, then execute C." If-then statements allow programmers to steer the computer in predetermined directions if certain variables present themselves.

We think about the future this way all the time. "If it rains tomorrow, we'll move the party indoors." "If we miss the bus, we'll catch a cab." If-then statements are the way we plan ahead, predict the outcome, and mentally prepare for whatever may arise.

Remember, though, that thinking about the future can only take place in the present moment. We can get so caught up in anticipating what's going to happen that we lose sight of what's actually happening. The future is an illusion; nothing happens until it happens.

Even at the highest levels of zen, our minds can slip off the track if we start thinking too far ahead. A story along these lines tells of the zen teacher Tekisui, who became ill while rebuilding a damaged temple. His disciple, Gasan, greeted him at his bedside.

The teacher asked, "What are you going to do when you get the temple rebuilt?"

"When your sickness is over we want you to speak there," Gasan said.

"Suppose I do not live until then?"

"Then we will get someone else," the disciple said.

"Suppose you cannot find anyone?"

"Don't ask such foolish questions!" said Gasan. "Just go to sleep."

We build our programs around if-then statements and plan

our lives the same way. But there is always an "if" we can't anticipate.

Then what?

Return to the present moment.

To ALL YOU programmers burning the midnight lamp: It's late. Get some sleep.

Bugs

As soon as we started programming, we found out to our surprise that it wasn't as easy to get programs right as we had thought. Debugging had to be discovered. I can remember the exact instant when I realized that a large part of my life from then on was going to be spent finding mistakes in my own programs.

—MAURICE WILKES, AUTHOR,
MEMOIRS OF A COMPUTER PIONEER

The hard work of programming begins with the rewriting—tracking down and fixing the flaws, or bugs, that keep a piece of software from running cleanly. One little typo in a long string of code can send a program crashing to a halt.

The debugging process demands testing and retesting in the

most thorough manner. Some programmers pursue this task more diligently than others. A few seem content to let users discover the bugs first. This shows a bug in their thinking.

Admittedly, a large, complex program may be impossible to fully debug until it's put through the full variety of day-to-day application, but many software products appear on the market with obvious bugs. Clearly, not all programmers take the time to check their work.

Zen requires a rigorous attitude toward debugging—to take responsibility for one's work and ensure that it's the best it can be. A life lived with passion shows itself in the concern for quality and attention to detail. If you don't care enough about your work to see that it's done right, why do the work? Poor-quality workmanship is a sign of a poor spirit.

Each of us experiences our own mental bugs, in which our thought process gets caught in a loop of apathy, negativity, and cynicism. Some bugs are minor and relatively easy to correct, while others take a lifetime of hard, persistent effort to squash. Either way, the first step in cleaning up a bug-filled mind is to shut down and restart. Consider the following two thought loops:

> *First thought:* I don't want to do this.
> *Second thought:* This job sucks.
> *Third thought:* I don't have time for this.
> *Fourth thought:* It's too much work for one person.
> *Fifth thought:* I'll deal with it tomorrow.

Sixth thought: It's not my fault.

Seventh thought: Let someone else worry about it.

SHUT DOWN

RESTART

First thought: Fix the problem.

Second thought: Do it right the first time.

Third thought: No whining, no excuses.

Fourth thought: I'm the one who's responsible.

Fifth thought: Make it sing.

Sixth thought: Let 'er rip.

Seventh thought: Next problem.

Once you commit to cleaning up the errors in your work, the errors in thinking take care of themselves.

Another thing: If the pressure of debugging starts getting to you, take a step back and look at the ant colonies under your feet—so organized and hard at work as they run around gathering food. Against the vastness of the universe, all our endeavors—our giant cities, roadways, industries, networks—are nothing more than these same little ant colonies.

Bugs, indeed. They're the most important things in the world, and the least.

May we pay attention to every last one.

Beta Version

I cannot believe that we are at the end of this story—we are not evolution's ultimate product. There's something coming after us, and I imagine it is something wonderful. But we may never be able to comprehend it, any more than a caterpillar can comprehend turning into a butterfly.

—DANNY HILLIS, FOUNDER,
THINKING MACHINES CORP.

The first draft of a computer program is called the alpha version. After an initial level of testing and debugging, the next draft is called the beta version.

Beta versions are the first versions that get put to the test in the real world. Like our lives, they're works in progress—not yet final, tangled with problems, in a state of becoming. We may refine our programs to the point of acceptance, but in zen, we're always in beta, even to the very end. The zen masters say *mi zai*: "Not yet." There is always more to learn, always another step up the mountain.

未在

Mi zai

Real-estate developers in New York City like to joke that theirs would be a great city if they could ever finish building it. In truth, though, a city can never finish building anymore than a software company can stand still with its current operating system or a chip maker can rest on its latest processor. There is always more to be done for tomorrow.

To be in beta is to be in the middle of a process—the process of *living*. The moment we stop testing, probing, improving, reworking, we stagnate and die.

Release

The opposite of a correct statement is a false statement.
The opposite of a profound truth may well be
another profound truth.

—Niels Bohr (1885–1962), Danish physicist

Software disseminated for general use is called a release. The time comes for everything and everybody to release, whether we like it or not.

So much of life is dominated by the fear of letting go. *My* money, *my* beliefs, *my* body—all spoken of as possessions. Yet in the end, what do we hold? Nothing.

Zen legend has it that when the Chinese master Hung-jen was ready to choose a successor, he asked the monks of the monastery to write a poem showing their level of zen awareness. The head monk, Shen-hsiu, wrote:

This body is the tree of enlightenment,
The mind is like a bright mirror standing;
Take heed to always keep it clean,
And allow no dust to ever cling.

Through zen, Shen-hsiu's poem says, we squarely face the challenge of letting go—of wiping the dust from our mirror. When jealousy arises, release. When hatred flares, release. When the child grows up, release. When the chariot swings low, release. Lay your burden down. Do not cling to anything.

But Shen-hsiu did not get picked to succeed his master. That honor went to a mere kitchen helper, Hui-neng, who replied to Shen-hsiu:

There never was a tree of enlightenment,
There never was a mirror shining bright;
Since there was nothing from the first,
Where, then, is the dust to cling?

Hui-neng's response showed an even deeper level of zen awareness than Shen-hsiu. The two men may have seemed to contradict each other, but both spoke the truth; Hui-neng's insight just cut deeper. In a sense, zen is like an onion, with many layers of truths. If Shen-hsiu's truth was on the level of 1, Hui-neng's was on the level of 0.

In 1, Shen-hsiu says, recognize your potential for enlightenment. Persevere in this life and release from all attachments.

In 0, Hui-neng says, awaken to the void at the source of all things, for it energizes this world of 1 we inhabit.

Now GO and work diligently on your program, testing and retesting, preparing for release. When the time comes, let it go like a child into the world. Your spirit goes with it.

Then start the work of upgrading. Your next release has to go even higher.

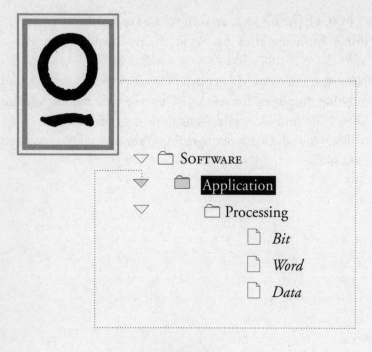

Application

One machine can do the work of fifty ordinary men. No machine can do the work of one extraordinary man.

—ELBERT HUBBARD, AUTHOR, *A MESSAGE TO GARCIA*

The reason we have a computer is to use it. Otherwise, the tool serves no purpose. What good would a computer be without its applications? Like a hammer with no nail to hit or a saw with no wood to cut.

We apply the machine to analyze, create, communicate, design, engineer, play games—whatever. To do so we must apply ourselves as well.

Nothing in zen comes through halfhearted effort. It demands the will to learn, improve, and do our best. The zen masters say *heiso ni ari:* ceaseless daily practice or, literally, "possess a calm, even base." That means we practice carrying a calm base all the time—walking, sitting, eating, and, yes, even sitting at the computer. Whether using the computer to create or communicate, process or play, we have to apply ourselves. To do otherwise is spiritless. Anytime you find your feet dragging, you're on the wrong path.

在平素

Zen is eminently practical in its application. Just be present in body, mind, and spirit; that is all. Some spiritually minded people can get too

Heiso ni ari

esoteric in their thinking. Once, a follower of the Tendai school of Buddhism approached the zen master Shinkan to discuss enlightenment. "Tendai claims that even the grass and trees will become enlightened," the man said.

"Of what use is it to discuss how grass and trees become enlightened?" Shinkan said. "The question is how you yourself can become so."

We answer Shinkan's question through ceaseless daily practice. Therein lies the ultimate application of zen: to carry on through the day and see zen anywhere we look. It is there in the flower held up wordlessly by the Buddha. It is there in every computer application. A single click of the mouse holds the ultimate realization. The truth inherent in one computer applies to myriad circumstances.

How to see it?

Apply yourself.

Processing

*We think computing ought to be
something that you don't even know you do.*

—SCOTT MCNEALY, CHAIRMAN, SUN MICROSYSTEMS

The fundamental nature of computing is to take an input and process it to produce an output. This describes the work of zen as well.

In computing, we think of input and output separately, as a yin-yang dichotomy. However, the way of zen lies in the middle, at the point where input and output merge. "Enter by form, exit from form," the zen masters say. We're always entering one moment and exiting to the next. The point is to be in the middle—not entering, not exiting, just *being*.

What matters on the path of spiritual development is *how* we do something—the process—rather than what that something is. Any action will be right so long as it is done as an expression of our pure selves, for it will be natural. If the means are right, the ends simply *are*. So whatever you do, do it the right way. *Do what has to be done, when it has to be done, as well as it can be done, and do it that way every time.* If you can follow that single rule, you will know zen.

We're such result-oriented people today that we consume ourselves with the output—the answer, the result, the finished product. We focus on the ends, unmindful of the means. We hear the results of surveys and polls, marketing studies and sales projections, rarely stopping to ask, how were these numbers produced?

On the path of spiritual growth, the crucial questions do not begin, "Who?" "What?" "Where?" "When?" or even, "Why?" They begin, "How?" These are the questions that uncover the process—the *way*.

The next time you sit down at the computer, examine how you do your work—not from a technical standpoint, but mentally and spiritually. Check your internal process. Then see what results.

Good input, good process—the output takes care of itself.

Bit

The soul of immensity dwells in minutiae.

—Jakob Bernoulli (1654–1705),
Swiss mathematician

bit is the tiniest amount of information a computer works with—a single binary digit. Each keystroke or mouse click sends an electronic signal to the computer rendered as a group of binary digits, 0s and 1s. Typically, the computer organizes these signals into bytes (a string of eight bits).

In some ways, a bit is much like what zen scholars call *nen.* Nen is a Japanese word meaning "unit of thought." The literal translation of nen is "the heart's spirit *in this very moment.*" In everyday usage, nen has the overtones of profound feeling, even religious conviction.

Nen

Zen philosophy sees the human thought process as divided into a complex interplay of nen, in the same way the computer works as a complex interplay of bits. When we experience something directly and immediately, that is considered the first nen—our core experience. For example, if a color were to come into our sight, we would grasp it wordlessly and intuitively as our first nen.

The second nen immediately follows. It becomes *aware* of

the first nen. We see a color (first nen) and our mind instantly registers that it has seen a color (second nen).

The third nen, and all those that follow, make up our stream-of-consciousness. They synthesize the preceding nen, analyzing, reasoning, commenting, fixating, puzzling, conceptualizing. Here is where word gets attached to experience. We see a color (first nen), become aware of seeing the color (second nen), and say, "That's a nice red. I wonder how it would look if I added a little blue to it?" (third nen). The ongoing interplay between first, second, and subsequent nen comprises the whole of our thoughts.

The challenge of zen practice is to prevent the second and third nen from cluttering the experience of the first—our direct, immediate perception of the world, our spontaneous laughter at the punchline of a joke. So often our minds get tangled up in their own thoughts and the first nen gets lost, the way a computer gets bogged down if it's trying to process too many data.

There are many times when we need to deal with complexity. But remember, at the core of complexity lies the clean and simple. When you think about it, everything in computing can be reduced to bits, each bit pure in its own right, part of the great flowing stream of processed data.

First bit, first nen. Everything else follows.

Word

The thoughts did not come in any verbal formulation.
I rarely think in words at all. A thought comes,
and I may try to express it in words afterward.

—ALBERT EINSTEIN (1879–1955)

One of the most common applications in computing today is word processing, the technology to make written words manipulable. We can cut, paste, and rearrange our phrases as we please, in a wide variety of formats and fonts.

Word processing makes it easy to write form letters, use boilerplate language, and fill in the blanks if we so choose. For all the speed and ease of technology, though, the essential element of word processing remains the *process*. What are we doing and how are we doing it? Do we care about our words? Are we choosing them wisely, putting them down in the right order, making them mean something? Are we being mindful?

Through zen, we seek to find that place of poetry where words go beyond the limits of words to evoke the indescribable. The highest priests of zen would use words to that effect even in the ordinary discourse of the day.

Once, the zen master Tozan was weighing some flax when a monk approached and asked, "What is Buddha?"

"Three pounds of flax," came the reply.

Tozan's phrase, one of the most famous in zen, may sound meaningless on the surface. Yet those were the words that sprang immediately out of his intuitive mind, his first nen, without any intellectual thought—an expression of pure soul and pure poetry. "Close were the words [to the ultimate truth]," noted the zen commentator Mumon, "but closer was the meaning." Tozan's words were like a finger pointing to the moon—showing the way to the beautiful light.

It may seem ludicrous to think of writing poetry when composing a simple memo or dashing off a note to someone. But the point is to be as mindful in these moments as in any other. Zen lies in the ordinary and the everyday—in weighing three pounds of flax. Just be natural; that is zen. As the master Nansen says, "Ordinary mind is the way."

More than emanating from our brains, words should spring from our hearts. Let the words follow the feeling. If you sign a letter, "Sincerely," be sincere.

Yes, the truth of zen lies beyond words, but it lives in every word as well. Process them mindfully.

Data

*Figures often mislead people. There is no shame in that:
words can mislead us as well. The problem with
numbers is our tendency to treat them with some
degree of awe, as if they are somehow more
reliable than words. . . . This belief is
wholly misplaced.*

—KEITH DEVLIN, PROFESSOR OF MATHEMATICS,
ST. MARY'S COLLEGE

omputers were born to crunch numbers—to process massive amounts of data and transform them into something meaningful. Data processing brings order to raw information by calculating, sorting, and uncovering patterns.

We rely on numbers for their sense of security; they have the feel of facts. There are times, however, when the truth lies behind and between the numbers.

The first challenge of data processing is to get good numbers. To even have a chance at a meaningful output, one must start with quality data, then process those data by asking the right questions. If the data are inaccurate, incomplete, or unrepresentative, the output will be unreliable—a process known in computer circles as "garbage in, garbage out." If what we ask of the data is biased, irrelevant, or unfocused, the output will be meaningless. As statisticians know, if you want a biased outcome, you can make the numbers say whatever you'd like.

Even if we get good numbers, the outcome can be inconclusive—ask any economist. Perhaps the numbers don't fit a pattern or they send contradictory signals. In such cases, only the intuition knows how to read them.

Zen demands a clear-eyed approach to data processing—to know what numbers can tell us and what they cannot. On the one hand, we know that numbers speak a universal language, that even the deepest reaches of space follow the laws of mathematics. On the other hand, no one in science can yet explain *why* the universe conforms to mathematical laws—where numbers *come from*. This is the ultimate mystery zen seeks to penetrate.

The data keep pouring in, overwhelming us. In the face of this information barrage, we'd do well to remember the words of zen master Daito Kokushi:

> *I beg you, try to find the fundamental source . . .*
> *Do not merely pinch off the leaves*
> *Or concern yourselves only with the branches.*

In the great scheme of things, most of the data we process amount to so many leaves and branches. The zen mind stays focused on the fundamental source, to be found in just two numbers, 0 and 1.

Discern the meaning of those two data, 0 and 1—the circle and the line—for therein lies the truth of all things.

Working With Files

It is a mathematical fact that the casting of this pebble from my hand alters the center of gravity of the universe.

—Thomas Carlyle (1795–1881)

In the metaphor of personal computing, the screen is a desktop and the hard drive is a filing cabinet. The work we do consists of files stored, retrieved, and discarded from the filing cabinet as needed.

From the mundane to the vital, each file is a discrete record of our thoughts and preoccupations, a mark of who we are and how we spend our time. The vast majority of files we view as banal, but every one we work on contains a little piece of our soul. Like the fingerpaintings of our childhood stored in the attic, these files tie us to a specific moment in time. They may be fascinating or wholly uninteresting. Either way, they are our creations.

Whatever you're working on, just be present in the moment; that is all. The record will speak for itself. Years later you can look back on your record and it will say, in the fullest sense:

I was here.

New

ew file, born empty.

What will become of it?

File Name

I believe in God, only I spell it Nature.

—FRANK LLOYD WRIGHT (1869–1959)

o computer file can exist without a name. From the moment it's born, it automatically receives a generic file name, such as "Untitled," until we give it a more specific name so as to remember its contents.

In naming a file, a subtle shift of consciousness takes place. No longer is the file anonymous; it has an identity. Like monks who enter a zen monastery, shedding their old names and receiving new ones to indicate spiritual rebirth, we give files a name to indicate their elevated status out of the untitled.

On one level, the name we give something does not matter. Call the flower a cherry blossom or a *sakura,* the bloom is no less brief or beautiful. Yet the name should harmonize with the spirit of the thing. We hear the names Frederick Austerlitz, Betty Joan Perske, Joe Yule Jr., and who can say what their lives would have been had they not come into the spotlight as Fred Astaire, Lauren Bacall, Mickey Rooney?

We encourage suffering people to call their feelings by names such as anger or sorrow in order to recognize their pain and begin the healing process. We even try to give a name to that which is unnameable—"God," "the Void," "the Way."

To name is human. It is the failure to name, or worse, failure to acknowledge a name, that leads us to become less human, less caring. How much easier is it to kill Jews in the Holocaust when their names become numbers tattooed on the arm? How much more do we ravage the environment when we don't know the names of all the species destroyed? How much more isolated do we become when we don't know the names of our neighbors?

The more we name the world around us, the more we recognize its glorious variety, and the more we connect ourselves within it. When we see the tree as a willow, the flower as a rose, the fish as a flounder, we see subdivisions within subdivisions that comprise the vast multitudes that make up the universe. We see that we, with our individual names, have our unique place in the multitudes, too.

That fresh new file on your screen, born "Untitled," is unlike any other file you've created—sole occupant of this moment— while at the same time united with all other files created the same way.

Name what can be named; align yourself with that which can't.

To this thinking, we give the name *zen*.

Folder

There is only one nature. The division into "science" and "engineering" is a human imposition, not a natural one. Indeed, the division is a human failure; it reflects our limited capacity to comprehend the whole.

—WILLIAM WULF, PROFESSOR
OF COMPUTER SCIENCE, UNIVERSITY OF VIRGINIA

On the computer, we organize our files into folders to help bring order to our thinking. Away from the machine, we compartmentalize our space and activities to help make sense of our lives. We have separate spaces for sleeping, bathing, eating, cooking, working, worshiping—a place for everything.

Zen asks that we recognize the folders within folders that make up our lives, yet transcend them at the same time. The truth is like music. We can break it down into categories, but at a certain point the effort becomes futile. Who can say what constitutes pop-jazz or jazz-rock? Ultimately, it's just music. But then comes the question, what is music? Is not music itself just another fuzzy category?

In one of zen's most famous questions, a monk asks the master Joshu, "Does a dog have a Buddha nature?" It's a straightforward yes or no question offering to put the dog in one of two folders.

Joshu's reply: "Mu."

Mu, in Japanese, means void or nothingness. Joshu is saying, put your mind above categories and toward the Great Void at the heart of all things. The either/or logic behind the monk's question is fundamentally flawed, Joshu says, because the truth transcends categorization; the answer is both yes *and* no, and neither yes *nor* no, all at the same time. We cannot say

Mu

"yes," because a dog does not have the human capacity for self-realization or enlightenment. Yet we cannot say "no," because a dog, like all creations, is a manifestation of the divine spirit.

On the computer, folders neatly compartmentalize our work, but all folders originate from the same source. So it is with each of us in life: All separate as individuals, yet all one in the great *uni*-verse.

Outside the window a dog barks.

Open

I keep the subject constantly before me and wait till the first dawnings open little by little into the full light.

—ISAAC NEWTON (1642–1727)

pen = 0 :

In the dictionary, it says

> *Accessible,*
> *Unrestricted,*
> *Spread out,*
> *Free to enter,*
> *Clear and unobstructed,*
> *Warm and inviting,*
> *Willing to listen,*
> *Generous of spirit—*
>
> *No endpoints.*

Open file, open mind.

Close

What we call the beginning is often the end
And to make an end is to make a beginning.
The end is where we start from.

—T. S. Eliot (1888–1965)

There is a time to close every file, just as there is a time to turn every page. Some closed files await reopening. Others vanish like a forgotten memory.

We all need closure in our lives. From closure is born a new beginning. Closure bends the 1, the straight line of time, and gives life dramatic arc—a sense of denouement.

Thus does the 1 cycle round and become a 0.

Print

The Way that is seen
Is not the true Way, until
You bring fresh toner.

—COMPUTER HAIKU, POSTED
ON THE INTERNET

When working within an application, we can revise and update a file as we please. But some information we like to have in a form to hold, pass around, mark up, fold, and carry. So we print it.

A hard-copy printout marks a piece of paper with information. These markings may be trivial or profound. Either way, the act of printing serves to document the file at a moment in time—as it *is*. In that moment, put yourself in the here and now.

The zen teacher Thich Nhat Hahn reminds us to see the tree and rainwater in every piece of paper. After all, nothing comes from nowhere. Rarely do we stop to consider the source of all the manufactured things in our lives. But they all have their origin in the elements.

Be mindful when you print—a record is being born into the physical world. Ask yourself why. Anything to which you give birth should serve a purpose.

Like the printed work you're holding . . .

Save

Half our life is spent trying to find something to do with the time we have rushed through life trying to save.

—WILL ROGERS (1879–1935)

Save early, save often.

No matter how many times we remind ourselves, we forget. We get caught up in a train of thought, the system crashes, and we lose part, if not all, of our work. The system manager can issue countless warnings but, in the end, individual users have to take responsibility to save their own files.

It's the same with saving souls. We all need to take care of our own work first. If you want to save the planet or save the human race, start by saving yourself from yourself—that is zen.

Forget to save and all may be lost.

Icon

It's not about charisma and personality, it's about results.

—STEVE JOBS, FOUNDER, APPLE COMPUTER

Icons are graphic representations of files, commands, or programs. We think nothing of moving these icons around, or even deleting them. They are mere symbols.

Zen takes a similar attitude. Most religions have icons deemed sacred; to destroy or treat them cavalierly would be unthinkable. But zen places no particular import on artifacts. Attachment of any kind, materially or otherwise, is to be avoided.

Legend has it that one zen master, thinking it too cold in a shrine, took a wooden Buddha off the mantle for use as fuel in the stove. The shrine keeper was horrified.

As the master poked around the ashes of the burned icon, the keeper said, "What are you looking for?"

"*Sariras,*" the master said, referring to small pebbles supposedly found in the ashes of saints after cremation.

"But you won't find them in the ashes of a wooden Buddha," the keeper said.

"In that case," the master said, "can I have the other two Buddhas for my fire?"

There is a zen saying, "If you meet the Buddha on your path, kill him." This is not to advocate the use of violence against sages. It means put your faith in yourself; kill the need to look for idols or gurus in the outside world. Zen puts all its faith in individual experience. Icons, relics, even the masters are unimportant compared with the disciplined pursuit of your own path.

The answer is not "out there." You already have it—just awaken to the fact.

The only icon is you.

Trash/Recycle

On the very campuses where mathematics is presented and received as an inhuman discipline, cold and dead, new mathematics is created. As sure as the tides.

—J. D. Phillips, author,
Geomorphic Systems

The trash or recycling bin is a holding area for files we think we don't need, until the time comes to reclaim the space they use.

As with your files, discard those things from your mind that take up unnecessary space—the fixations, obsessions, and distractions. It's easy for memory to become filled with regrets, an unrequited love, the roads not taken. We have to clear those thoughts out and create room for new ones. Let go. Empty your cup and keep it empty.

On the other hand, recycle those thoughts worth saving—the mantras and reminders that keep us focused on the path. When feeling down, as everyone does sometimes, the way back up is through reminding ourselves of the truths we already know. Once on the positive cycle, stay there.

Trash and move on: That is living in 1.
Recycle and use again: That is living in 0.
Either way is zen.

Quit

In the midst of all this paper sat Alsing's computer terminal. On the screen of the tube in white letters, like the little voice that whispers in a wild gambler's ear, this message stood:

ARE YOU SURE YOU WANT TO QUIT NOW?

—TRACY KIDDER, AUTHOR,
THE SOUL OF A NEW MACHINE

The way of zen is to persevere. Even in perseverance, though, there's a time to exit.
Take a break.
Relax, regroup, refocus.
Begin again.
Same mountain, further up.

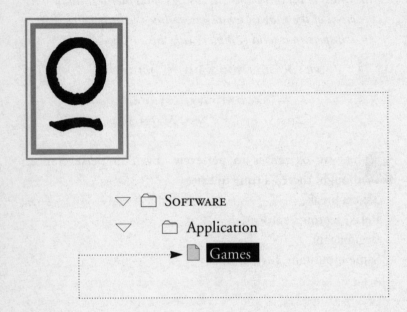

Games

My work is a game, a very serious game.

—M. C. ESCHER (1898–1970), DUTCH ARTIST

W hen the world champion of chess, Gary Kasparov, lost a six-game match to the IBM computer Deep Blue in 1996, the outcome befuddled him. "It is very difficult to analyze the results of the match," he told *The New York Times*. "I know what I did wrong, but I don't know what the computer did right or wrong. It's a mystery."

On some level, solving that mystery is what drives every computer-game player, no matter what the game or skill level. All computer games, by the nature of their construction, have a logic built into them. They follow strict written instructions, programmed from the outset. Decipher the logic of the game and the designer's intent and, once you hone your skill, you can beat the machine. The player's quest is to achieve a meeting of the minds with the programmer.

Zen is like this, too. Through practice in the game of life, we seek a similar meeting of the minds—of mind with Mind, aligning ourselves with the way of life's Great Programmer. The mystery of life eludes us, but we play on, guided by our glimpses at the truth.

As in life, many computer games can leave us without a clue as to what's going on. We have to figure out the rules for ourselves, learning through trial and error what moves lead to trouble or safety. Surprises come from nowhere to throw us off balance. Crises arise that demand immediate attention. These characteristics of games heighten our sense of mindfulness. No serious player would call computer games a mindless activity; quite the opposite. The level of concentration can be so high it leads to a meditative state.

The physical aspects of playing computer games can lead us to zen as well. Some games move so fast they require mind-body coordination on the level of the martial arts. Through practice, we build muscle memory to the point where thought and action occur simultaneously. The hand learns what to do and moves not from the mind's direction, but from intuition.

Some games one does not play so much as immerse into. The programmer creates an artificial world with its own logic and reality, in which the player has a specific role to play. Like actors on a stage, players of these games face a zen paradox: They realize they're pretending, yet they take that pretending seriously, investing the whole of their spirit and emotions.

The problem for computer-game players is when they lose the delicate balance between control and addiction. The mindful player retains the ability in total concentration to stand above the moment—to recognize the point where continued play arises out of obsession, not enjoyment.

Let computer games be a teacher, not a ruler.

HERE ARE Zen Computer's Five Rules of Playing Computer Games:

1. Set aside time to play.

There is a time to work and a time to play. Make sure to find the proper yin-yang balance. Too much time working is unhealthy, as is too much time playing.

Sometimes work is a game; sometimes a game is work. If the game doesn't give you enjoyment, find something else to take its place, whether on the computer or off.

Make time for fun—it's called living.

2. Care.

Game or no game, in everything you do, your approach matters. Put your heart into it and give it your best effort. When you can hold your head high, winning and losing do not matter.

If you do not care about your performance and do not give good effort, you are wasting your time and the time of those who want to play.

Know the difference between playing to win and playing not to lose. Playing to win is letting go; playing not to lose is holding on. The way of zen is through letting go.

Understand, too, the true nature of victory. "Playing to win" does not mean "win at all costs." Sometimes there is winning in losing. Let the child come out on top. Lose the battle, win the war.

Life cannot be tallied on a scoreboard.

3. Play fair.

The rules of a game should foster competition, strategy, and fairness. Play within that spirit.

Often people seek to exploit the rules to unfair advantage. In unfairness there is imbalance. The way of zen is through balance. Practice to maintain it.

So many times, in so many ways, we don't even play fair with ourselves. We cheat at playing solitaire, both literally and figuratively. We look for shortcuts, ignoring our better judgment.

We all have an inner referee. Listen to the whistle.

4. Learn from every contest.

Every game presents an opportunity to learn—about the game, the competitors, and ourselves.

Sometimes we learn what to do next time.

Sometimes we learn what not to do next time.

Sometimes we learn there is no next time—only now.

Let the game teach you. Then take what you learn and apply it elsewhere.

From one thing, know ten thousand things.

5. Master the inner game.

The game within the game is the only game that matters. How we handle success and how we handle failure determines our progress in life.

As the samurai say, "The only opponent is within." Battle hard, because—*especially* with the inner game—

It ain't over till it's over.

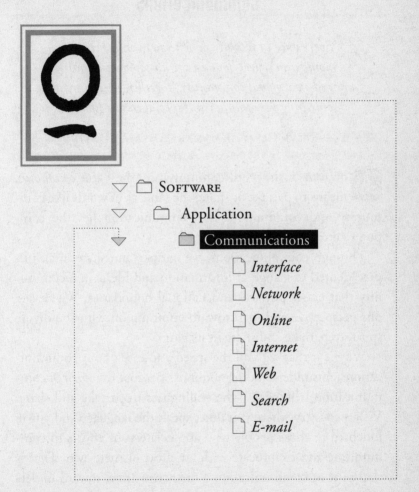

▽ 📁 SOFTWARE
▽   📁 Application
▽   📁 **Communications**
         📄 *Interface*
         📄 *Network*
         📄 *Online*
         📄 *Internet*
         📄 *Web*
         📄 *Search*
         📄 *E-mail*

Communications

*Every once in a while, when you're online, take a
moment to reflect how we are all pioneers building
a brand-new global community. Together, we are creating
something very unique and special in our lifetime.*

—STEVE CASE, CHAIRMAN, AMERICA ONLINE

T he root of the word communicate, the Latin *communis,*
means to partake or share, the same as in words like community and communion. In communication lies the computer's great promise.

Through communications, we partake and share in an unprecedented exchange of information and ideas, in a community that erases physical and national boundaries. We elevate our perspective and inch toward communion with the divine spirit, to partake and share in its glory.

Why is it that with all the speed and ease of our communications, misunderstanding abounds? Because the *spirit* of communication is missing—the willingness to partake and share. Visit a country where you don't speak the language and you're indebted to those people who appreciate your efforts to communicate and reciprocate with an effort of their own. That is the spirit of communication—the active effort toward understanding.

So often, we think the path of spiritual growth requires retreat from the world. Indeed, the history of zen is rife with examples of hermit monks. While we all need time to be alone with our thoughts, the true way of zen demands partaking in the community and sharing with others. The zen master Kakuan says the point beyond enlightenment is simply to be "in the world," going to the marketplace and mingling, sharing what one has learned. "I visit the wineshop and the market," he says, "and everyone I look upon becomes enlightened."

As humans, we can never hope to communicate as precisely as computers with their yin-yang data stream of 0s and 1s. But if the spirit is there, we can communicate the incommunicable—through what's said, what's unsaid, what's between the lines. Such is the art of communication—and the zen of it.

Interface

Number proceeds from unity.

—ARISTOTLE (384–322 B.C.)

An interface is the connecting point between two separate things. It could be the connecting point between, say, two different computer systems. Or it could be the connecting point between the computer and the human user. In any case, an interface represents the junction where two separate entities become one.

Anytime two become one, zen is there. In a riddle that the masters ask, zen students are instructed to ponder, "What was your original face before you were born?"

Today one might answer, "Look! The interface between computer and printer, right here."

It follows: Two become one, 1 becomes 0.

Network

When you go to Office Depot to buy a fax machine, you are not just buying a US$200 box. You are purchasing for $200 the entire network of all other fax machines and the connections between them—a value far greater than the cost of all the separate machines.

—KEVIN KELLEY, EXECUTIVE EDITOR, *WIRED*

The power of modern computing lies not only in the capability of each machine, but in the connections the machines make to each other. When linked together in a company, a school, or, more broadly, on the Internet, computers can share information instantly across physical boundaries.

Thus, when you buy a computer, you're not only buying a machine that can perform certain functions for you. You're buying access to a whole network of other computers. By joining the network, you add to the value of all the other machines in the group. In other words, as the number of units in a network rises arithmetically, the value of the network rises exponentially.

Zen may be a solitary pursuit, but following its path adds value to the network of human relations. Like ripples in a pool, the work of self-cultivation emanates outward. Thus can Kakuan say, "Everyone I look upon becomes enlightened." Those who elevate their own humanity inspire others to do the same.

So it can be said that in the vast network of the modern age, a single person can change the world:

You.

Online

*The idea of a continuum seems simple to us. We have somehow
lost sight of the difficulties it implies.*

—Erwin Schrodinger (1887–1961),
Austrian theoretical physicist

To be online is to be connected, via modem to the Internet
or between devices such as computer and printer. A
pipeline has been opened up for communication.

Zen means to go online as well—to make a connection outside of ourselves and open up to communication. Once online,
stay on *line*. That is, follow the one true path, step by step, until it is time to log off.

Online is
one line is
1.

Internet

*Any medium powerful enough to extend man's reach is powerful
enough to topple his world. To get the medium's magic to work
for one's aims rather than against them is to attain literacy.*

—ALAN KAY, COMPUTER SCIENTIST, DEVELOPER OF OBJECT-
ORIENTED SOFTWARE TECHNOLOGY

From its origins in the U.S. defense system, the Internet
has grown organically to become the largest of all computer networks—global, decentralized, anarchic, still evolving.
No one controls it; it has no governing body and no laws. We
don't know what shape it will ultimately take, or how it will ultimately affect our lives. That's the zen of it: We're making it up
as we go along.

Many people mistakenly think of the Internet as a destination but, like zen, it is merely a pathway. As the zen masters say,
"Don't ask where the path is. You're on it." In every step and
every moment, where you go is up to you. We can choose to
read the news from across the country, chitchat with a group of
far-flung strangers, research the minutiae of a government re-
port, go wherever our curiosity leads. Never before has so much
information or such a vast community been available without
one having to leave the home.

Yet all of that means nothing if we fail to develop the basic qualities of wisdom, responsibility, and trustworthiness.

We must be wise enough to help those who seek the pathway find their way onto it, and to make the world of cyberspace secure without compromising freedom.

We must be responsible enough to handle the freedom cyberspace offers, respecting the privacy of others.

We must remember that in a world of anonymity, entered through aliases, trustworthiness, credibility, and integrity still matter.

WE BUILD THESE elements of character through training in zen. The Japanese call the place for such training a *dojo*. Literally, dojo means "place of the Way," the great Way of the universe. A dojo can be any place you make it, so long as the spirit of training is there. What makes a dojo special is not its location or physical characteristics, but the student's behavior in it.

道
場

Dojo

Think of the Internet as a dojo. Together, with likeminded users of Zen Computer, we make a shared commitment to the dojo as *our* place, a place to help each other grow. Then, when the question is asked, "Where do you want to go today?" you can answer:

Right here, right now.

Web

The Web was built by millions of people simply because they wanted it, without need, greed, fear, hierarchy, authority figures, ethnic identification, advertising, or any other form of manipulation. Nothing like this ever happened before in history. We can be blasé about it now, but it is what we will be remembered for. We have been made aware of a new dimension of human potential.

—Jaron Lanier, composer and computer scientist who coined the term *virtual reality*

The World Wide Web is the fastest-growing part of the Internet, the graphical face of the information superhighway. The central feature of the Web is its use of hypertext, a system that allows for creative links between information. Through hypertext, information can be organized nonsequentially, according to the user's associative train of thought. Those links can lead anywhere on the Web, creating a gigantic nexus of information.

The World Wide Web vividly illustrates the idea that we are, indeed, all linked, not only to each other but to the One Great Source as well. For the very root of the word religion, the Latin *religio,* means "linking back." Through the Web, we remind ourselves of *religio* with every click on every link.

"The many have one essence," the sages say, "and the one has many manifestations." Put another way, every wave is of the ocean, and the ocean produces many waves.

Now surf the Web.

Search

The Web site you seek
cannot be located but
endless others exist

—COMPUTER HAIKU
POSTED ON THE INTERNET

In order to find something on the Internet, you typically have to search for it. With certain software, you can type in a few key words to identify your area of interest and, *voilà,* you get a list of sites that match your criteria. Some of the sites may turn out to have nothing to do with your inquiry; others will tell you more than you need to know. But if it's information you want, it's information you'll get.

Enlightenment is an altogether different matter. Zen masters say, "If you seek it, you will not find it." We can search our whole lives for something, never realizing we already have it. We will never be able to find the ultimate It, because It is beyond finding; we're of It and ultimately *are* It.

Search for what you need to know.
Awaken to what you already are.

E-mail

To: you@here.now
Subj: from 1 to 0

every message creates a line—1.
every reply creates a loop—0.
please keep in touch. may the circle be unbroken.

sincerely,

<send now>

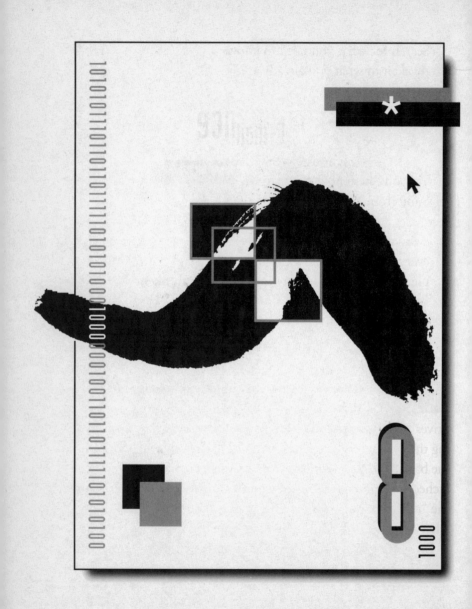

8
1000

Maintenance

What goes up must come down.
Ask any system administrator.

—Anonymous, posted on the Internet

T HERE IS NOTHING glamorous about maintenance. Cleaning out files, compressing folders, formatting backup drives—all these mundane activities take time away from using the computer to achieve our ends. As anyone who works in the back office of a company knows, there's a certain stigma attached to maintenance, as though it's somehow a lesser job than the "real" work of the firm. But maintenance enables us to do what we want. Without it, we'd collapse.

Everything needs maintenance, from machines to homes to

our bodies to this very earth. The more we avoid it, the more we allow problems to build up. Those in the medical profession know that it's far more costly to society when a patient waits until needing emergency care rather than getting a preventative checkup.

Zen, too, is all in the upkeep. There's nothing glamorous about zen. Its way can be known through maintenance alone.

I once visited a karate school in New York City, located in a converted warehouse. The entrance had a heavy iron door. Inside, the first four floors were dark, musty, and filled with industrial machinery. On the landing of the fourth floor, the steps in front of me suddenly brightened. The wood on the staircase had been meticulously polished. As I entered the training hall at the top of the stairs, the whole room had the same spotless look. The wooden floor glowed; the mirrored walls gleamed spotlessly. I watched the training session and saw why. At the conclusion of the class, no one left. Every student grabbed a rag and began hand-polishing the floor and walls. They repeated the same ritual after every session.

In zen, to sweep the floor is to sweep the soul. Through maintenance, we show concern for what we have, and for our surroundings. How many of us feel a sense of accomplishment after a good spring cleaning? We can give our whole attention over to getting out a tough stain, pulling the weeds, or washing the windows. Cleaning helps to focus the mind.

The main attitude of zen maintenance is to take care of

things *before* a problem shows up. Be in the moment, but use the moment to think ahead as well.

Zen Computer's Three Rules of Maintenance:

1. Dust before you see dust.

At the karate school I visited, students wiped down the mirrors even when the glass looked immaculate. They gave no chance for dust to accumulate. They did not think, "It's already clean." Their mindset was, "Keep it clean." As Shen-hsiu wrote, "Allow no dust ever to cling." The same is true in computers. Run the antivirus program before you have a virus. Wipe the screen down before you see dust.

2. Clean as you go.

Some cooks prepare their meals and leave a big mess in the kitchen to be dealt with later. Others clean as they go, disposing of waste, rinsing things down, putting spices away after their use *as part of the process* of cooking.

"Maintenance" is not a separate category from "work." Don't wait for the mess to get bigger, or it will become that much harder to deal with. If we leave maintenance for later, the hard drive becomes fragmented and runs slower; the computer disk gets filled with data we can't even remember we saved. Delete needless files right away, instead of saving them to get trashed whenever.

Zen is one continuous path, so polish it with each step.

3. A place for all things, and all things in their place.

One reason we have stacks of paper on our desk, or toys all over the floor, or can't find our keys, is because we've yet to determine a place to put them. Make folders to store the files; get a toybox for the toys; pound a nail in the wall to hang the keys.

Once we have a place to put things, the challenge is to put them away. Keep the desk clean, pick up the toys, hang up the keys. When you're done with something, put it back where you got it, so it's there for the next time. If you borrow a disc from a colleague, remember to return it. It's so simple. That's why it's so hard.

HERE ARE a few files to consider within the folder of maintenance:

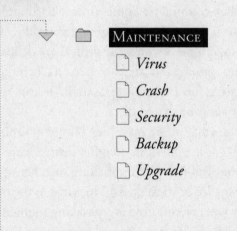

MAINTENANCE

Virus

Crash

Security

Backup

Upgrade

Virus

*There is no permanent place in
the world for ugly mathematics.*

—GODFREY H. HARDY (1877–1947),
AUTHOR, *A MATHEMATICIAN'S APOLOGY*

A computer virus is a purposely destructive piece of software code, often hidden in a tainted file that gets passed along to other computers. Some viruses flash annoying messages on your screen, others can corrupt your files or crash your machine. Programmers who write viruses are deliberately seeking to inflict damage on another person's computer system. Once a virus is in a computer system, it can easily spread through networks or shared discs.

These viruses may attack machines, but they are born of a virus in the mind—of the intent to do other people harm. Some people have ideological reasons for inflicting such harm; others do it out of sheer malice or wickedness. This virus in the mind may lie dormant for years or consume every waking moment. But, once it surfaces, how quickly it can spread from one user to the next.

Zen knows there will never be the perfect antibody for this virus in the mind. Within yin and yang, there is always a measure of sickness within health. Through zen, we walk the difficult path toward compassion—doing all we can to rid ourselves of the virus, finding the way to live in harmony with those who spread it around us.

When faced with a computer virus, first take aggressive steps to counteract it. Second, see the malice inherent in those viruses and counterbalance it with compassion.

Which action takes more effort?

Crash

A crash reduces
your expensive computer
to a simple stone.

—Computer haiku,
posted on the Internet

A computer is said to crash when it completely stops working. The picture on the screen freezes; the pointer stops moving; typing on the keyboard produces nothing. Whatever work the user hasn't saved may be lost.

In work or in life, no one wants to face an abrupt ending, but we live with the possibility all the time. Every time we buckle our seat belt or save a file in mid-thought, we're acknowledging that a crash might be out there.

Be mindful of that the next time you unbuckle your seat belt. You've arrived safely. Give thanks.

Security

To conquer fear is the beginning of wisdom, in the pursuit of truth as in the endeavor after a worthy manner of life.

—BERTRAND RUSSELL (1872–1970)

Computer security aims to protect data from theft, destruction, or viewing by unauthorized users. Specific security measures may include encrypting the data or issuing secret passwords to users who want access to a network.

We all want to feel safe in an unsafe world, protected from danger, at ease in our skin—there is no longing more basic to the human soul. We try to build the best security systems, but in the end, the potential for a breach will always exist. A single violation can bring our sense of security crashing down. In fact, that is one of the reasons we turn to zen.

Once, when a new monk entered a zen monastery and proclaimed no fear of death, the master replied, "Then you will not go far in zen."

Zen asks us to face our fears directly, to "make a friend of fear." Through training, students don't seek to eliminate their fears so much as to recognize and accept them. The idea is to transform fear from an overwhelming opponent into a well-known part of ourselves, put in its proper place.

The need for security should always be balanced against the need for personal freedom. Law enforcers tell us we can develop a security system strong enough to eliminate terrorism—but it wouldn't be the kind of world in which we'd want to live. Similarly, we can strengthen the security of our computer networks to the point where we lose the freedom of information.

The way to balancing is through zen. We will never find that place of total security, whether protecting data on the Internet or on the computers of the Defense Department. However, it's far better to have an open society with some elements closed than a closed society with some elements open. There will always be a small spot of yin within the yang—the rogue few who seek to spoil the interests of the many. All we can do in zen is put that insecurity in its place.

Therein lies the first step toward security.

Backup

The most likely way for the world to be destroyed, most experts agree, is by accident. That's where we come in; we're computer professionals. We cause accidents.

—NATHANIEL BORENSTEIN, AUTHOR,
"PROGRAMMING AS IF PEOPLE MATTERED"

In computing, we create backup copies of our files just in case something happens to the original. All machines break down at some point, so the safe course of action is to have a backup. As it says in the Seven Rules of Zen Computer, "Expect the unexpected."

The same reminder goes here. (Just backing it up.)

P.S. Save early, save often.

Upgrade

Software suppliers are trying to make their software packages more "user-friendly" . . . Their best approach, so far, has been to take all the old brochures and stamp the words "user-friendly" on the cover.

—BILL GATES, CHAIRMAN, MICROSOFT

A computer upgrade is, as the name implies, a new version of a product designed to replace the old one. From computers to laundry detergent to personal growth, few promises sell like the notion of "new and improved."

A good upgrade improves deficiencies and, more important, retains the best of what was. Not all upgrades fulfill their promise. Some are gimmicks, some are inconsequential, some replace old problems with new problems.

In products or in life, the only upgrade that matters is the one resulting from hard work and sincere effort at improvement. Better is not change for change's sake; better is *better.*

Zen Computer holds out the possibility of upgrading your life every time you turn on the machine. In the paradox of zen, it does so by showing that the way to upgrading your life is through realizing *there is no upgrading of your life.* Your life is what it is. The task is to *awaken* to what it is—what it *is.* Once you do that, you realize there can be no upgrading, because nothing can be better than what is.

If you want a way toward something better, just be. Zen is not a thing that makes a new you.

It makes you *you*.

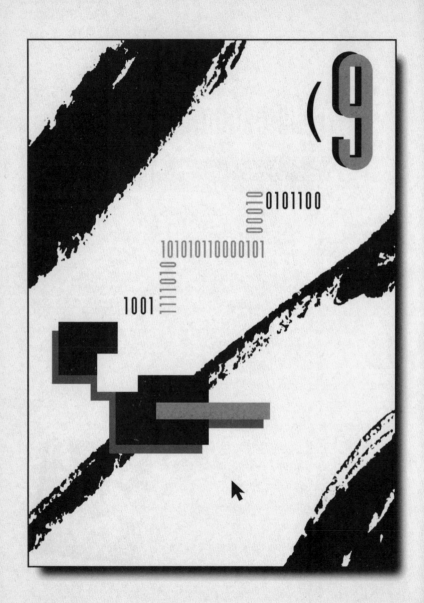

Troubleshooting Guide

Fixing Zen Computer

Beware of programmers who carry screwdrivers.

—Quote displayed on Unix fortune program,
attributed to Leonard Brandwein

T HIS CHAPTER PROVIDES solutions to common problems experienced by beginning computer users. In most cases, the answer doesn't lie with technical support. It lies within.

The computer doesn't turn on.

Check to make sure the computer is plugged in. That is, begin at the beginning: Locate the source of energy and let it flow through the computer.

I repeat: Find the energy source. Let it flow through the computer.

The cable is not the sole conduit.

The computer is turned on but the screen is dark.

Check to make sure the monitor is turned on. If not, flip the switch that turns on the light. It's the toggle between 0 (off) and 1 (on). There, in that one switch, lies the radiance.

If you're sensing the light but still can't see it, try closing your eyes. Some people find the way through smell, some through sound, some through taste, some through feel. The light comes to us in myriad ways.

The pointer doesn't move when you move the mouse.

Check to see if the mouse is plugged into the computer and that everything in your system is connected. What you're experiencing—the pointer not moving when you move the mouse—indicates some kind of disconnection. It could be a simple line disconnection or a deeper disconnection between mind and body and thought and action.

Zen Computer is a system aimed at fusing all component parts into one. If everything's connected properly, the hand and eye act as one system—mouse and pointer move together *as one.* If you perceive a lag between the two, you have to rebalance yourself and find a new sense of coordination.

Remember, too, that the way to the truth never varies. Like a finger pointing to the moon, the pointer doesn't move from the ultimate destination.

Typing on the keyboard produces nothing on the screen.

Check to make sure the keyboard is plugged into the computer. If it is connected, then perhaps by *nothing* you mean your keyboard work produces nothing of worth. This is the hard, slow work of zen. You have to persevere through times when it seems like nothing is happening and no growth is taking place. If you're doing your work, you have to trust that it will result in later gains. Be patient. It will.

So often in zen study students hear stories of the masters gaining sudden enlightenment, at something so simple as the call of a bird. These stories omit the years of hard training that preceded the decisive moment. Keep working: In zen, you have to find the place where nothing is also something. On the surface it may seem like nothing's happening, but you must trust that your inner work is getting done.

Then again, perhaps by *nothing* you mean no tangible thing—that, in typing, you don't produce anything to hold, you just rearrange the electrons on your screen into new shapes. Just remember this about those electrons on the screen: Your spirit is in them, right there on the screen. Like those electrons, your spirit, too, is no tangible thing, and yet visible in every word and action.

Or perhaps by *nothing* on the screen, you mean an expression of complete emptiness—a haiku in touch with the deepest source of inspiration. Imagine that—every keystroke you type, leading to the void.

Pure poetry.

.

The pointer freezes on the screen.

The pointer freezing on your screen means your system has crashed. Restart your computer.

We don't want the computer to freeze in mid-action any-more than we ourselves would want to freeze. But sometimes in the way of nature, the deer gets caught in the headlights. In those moments when the computer freezes, we may lose an important file or an important connection. No matter how much we want to hold on to what was there, we have to let go and restart. If we can do that—let go freely, with no clinging—we ascend to a higher place.

Out of freezing, into flowing.

Your program quits unexpectedly.

Who can say why a program quits with no warning? Not even the system's creators always know for certain.

Some things in this universe defy explanation. Scientists doggedly pursue the answers, trying to discern the way through reason. But zen knows the essence of Mind cannot be known, formulated, or understood by mere mind. "The sword cannot cut itself," the masters say; it is one thing, just as our minds are one with Mind. Mind is the sword; our feeble mind tries to cut the sword. The effort is futile. We cannot get out of mind to know Mind.

The sages know that God, the Source, the Way—whatever name you give it—lies beyond human comprehension, that even to assign a name to it puts our mind in the limited realm of language. "The Way that can be named is not the nameless Way," they say. "The Way that can be known is not the unknowable Way."

Trying to find the ultimate answer through rational means is like halving halves infinitely. As small as a half gets, there is always more to reduce. The process of scientific inquiry is the same. Even with all our avenues of specialization, halving the halves in the field of knowledge, the effort to explain scientifically why the unexpected sometimes happens will eventually lead in a circle. Let that circle teach us something. When every thread of logic leads to the point of, "I know not," *as it has to,* find the place where questioning ends and acceptance begins.

Ultimately, there is no *why* and no *because.* There just *is.* Make way and accept. Affirm with enlightened eyes.

Your computer can't find the printer.

Check the manual to see if you've followed the proper procedures for hooking the printer to the computer.

As technical support people know, a lot of computer questions can be answered by simply looking through the manual. But many users never read the manual.

We all have to figure things out for ourselves in this life. But how often do we veer off into "new" discoveries only to learn that ten thousand people have already been there? So much has been left to us by the great *senseis*—the ones who have gone before. It's all written down in the books. Even though we have to discover the truth for ourselves, we forget sometimes that the sages are there to help us.

Granted, a lot of manuals are poorly written, making it hard for people to find or understand the answer. But in the great books of instruction, the answer will be right there, and you will understand it.

One book can show you the way.

The printer won't print.

First, give the printer a good whack. It's amazing how often the primitive approach works with finicky hardware.

If all else fails, do not neglect the older technologies available. The pencil can always act as toner to your hand printer.

In the midst of complexity, do not forget the power of simplicity.

Printing takes a long time.

It does if you think it does. Time is relative. If you don't think printing takes a long time, then it doesn't take a long time.

Zen is known through the latter feeling. Learn to conquer haste and live with delayed gratification.

Mi zai, the masters say: "Not yet."

Shut Down

Nature is an infinite sphere of which the center is everywhere and the circumference nowhere.

—BLAISE PASCAL (1623–62)

1 = ON

0 = OFF

When the day is done,

Go to your resting place.

Empty everything—

No work, no play

No nothing.

Turn 1 to 0:

Line into circle.

Sleep in the arms of the Great Mother,

Dream under the gaze of the Great Father.

In love, the two will make one again—

Through you, who smiles

The contented smile of a newborn,

Awakened.

Select Bibliography

Aitken, Robert. *The Gateless Barrier: The We-Men Kuan (Mumonkan)*. San Francisco: North Point Press, 1990.

Boa, Fraser. *The Way of Myth: Talking with Joseph Campbell*. Boston: Shambhala, 1994.

Campbell, Joseph with Bill Moyers. *The Power of Myth*. New York: Doubleday, 1988.

Ching, Tsai Chih. *Zen Speaks: Shouts of Nothingness*. Trans. by Brian Bruya. New York: Anchor Books Doubleday, 1994.

Deng Ming-Dao. *365 Tao: Daily Meditations*. New York: Harper San Francisco, 1992.

Frankl, Victor E. *Man's Search for Meaning*, 4th ed. Boston: Beacon Press, 1959.

Grigg, Ray. *The New Lao Tzu*. Rutland, Vt.: Charles E. Tuttle, 1995.

Grigg, Ray. *The Tao of Zen*. Rutland, Vt.: Charles E. Tuttle, 1989.

Hanh, Thich Nhat. *Peace Is Every Step*. New York: Bantam Books, 1991.

Humphreys, Christmas. *Zen: A Way of Life*. Lincolnwood, Ill.: NTC Publishing Group, 1992.

Kaye, Les. *Zen at Work*. New York: Crown Trade Paperbacks, 1996.

Lao Tzu. *The Way of Life*. Trans. R. B. Blakney. New York: Mentor, 1955.

Leggett, Trevor. *A First Zen Reader*. Rutland, Vt.: Charles E. Tuttle Co. Inc., 1960.

Reps, Paul. *Zen Flesh, Zen Bones*. New York: Anchor Books, 1961.

Sekida, Katsuku. *Two Zen Classics*. New York: Weatherhill, 1977.

Sen, Soshitsu XV. *Tea Life, Tea Mind*. New York: Weatherhill, 1979.

The Shambhala Dictionary of Buddhism and Zen. Boston: Shambhala, 1991.

Shimano, Eido Tai, and Kogetsu Tani. *Zen Word, Zen Calligraphy*. Boston: Shambhala, 1990.

Strand, Clark. *Seeds from a Birch Tree: Writing Haiku and the Spiritual Journey*. New York: Hyperion, 1997.

Sudo, Philip Toshio. *Zen Guitar*. New York: Simon & Schuster, 1997.

Suzuki, D. T. *An Introduction to Zen Buddhism*. New York: Grove Press, 1964.

Wienpahl, Paul. *The Matter of Zen*. New York: New York University Press, 1964.

Quotation Sources

Most of the quotes in this book came from online sources. Particularly helpful were:

Platonic Realms Quotes Collection:
http://www.mathacademy.com/platonic_realms/quotes/Quotfram.html

>   Aristotle
>   Jakob Bernoulli
>   Scott Buchanan
>   Susan Gerhart
>   Godfrey H. Hardy
>   William James
>   Bernard Le Bovier Fontenelle
>   Isaac Newton
>   J. D. Phillips
>   Erwin Schrodinger

Mathematical Quotations, Furman University:
http://naturalscience.com/dsqhome.html

>   János Bolyai
>   Carl Jacobi
>   Albert Einstein (Word)
>   Thomas Carlyle
>   Blaise Pascal (Option, Pixel, Shut Down)

Another excellent online source was Michael Moncur's Quotations Page:
http://www.starlingtech.com/quotes/

>   Isaac Asimov
>   Pablo Picasso
>   Nathaniel Borenstein

Andy Rooney
Elbert Hubbard
B. F. Skinner

Using Moncur's search engine, I also located the following:

Cole's Quotables:
Lee Iacocca

alt.quotations archives:
Joseph Weizenbaum

USENET fortune file:
Alan Kay

Poor Man's College quote collection:
Alfred A. Montapert

Gabriel Robins also maintains a quotations page at
http://www.cs.virginia.edu/~robins, where I found quotes for:

Albert Einstein (Space Bar)
Niels Bohr
René Descartes
Antoine de Saint-Exupéry
William Wulf

Another helpful source was Quoteland: http://www.quoteland.com/index.html:

C.A.R. Hoare
Leonard Brandwein
Maurice Wilkes
Anonymous (Maintenance)

"Computer Related Quotes": http://www.rbdc.com/~bdot/quote3.html:
    Bill Gates
    Turnaucka's Law

http://www.dgp.toronto.edu/~accot/English/Hobbies/Citations.html:
    Chinese proverb
    Arthur C. Clarke
    Frank Lloyd Wright

"The Meaning of Hack," as well as other interesting insights into hacker culture and slang, can be found at The Jargon File: http://www.it.com.au/jargon/

The computer haiku I found at:

    http://www.savageresearch.com/humor/ComputerHaiku.html

Other online sources of quotes:

Steve Jobs: "There's Sanity Returning," online-only version of *Business Week* Q&A, May 25, 1998 (www.apple.com)
Esther Dyson: http://www.Release2-0.com/
Michael Budiansky: http://developer.apple.com/features/quadfeature1.html
Sherry Turkle: "I 'R US: Rethinking Identity With Sherry Turkle," by Robert Atkins: http://talkback.lehman.cuny.edu/tb/centersherryturkle.html
Albert Einstein (If-then): http://meyer.fys.ku.dk/~raben/einstein/
M.C. Escher: http://www.lane.k12.or.us/districts/junctioncity/JCHS/quote/97/05/index.html
Elliot Smorodinsky: http://www.cs.kuleuven.ac.be/~nico/fortune/apr1997.frt
Eric Hoffer: http://zia.hss.cmu.edu/miller/teaching/quotes.html
Steve Case: Newsletter to America Online subscribers, May 8, 1998
Scott McNealy: Keynote Address, Consumer Electronics Show, Las Vegas, Nev., Jan. 12, 1998, http://wwwseast2.usec.sun.com/corporateoverview/news/ces.html

Other quotes came from the following print sources:

The Oxford Dictionary of Modern Quotations, Tony Augarde, ed., Oxford University Press, 1991:
- George Orwell
- George Bernard Shaw
- T. S. Eliot
- Will Rogers
- Bertrand Russell

Keith Devlin: *The Universe and the Teacup: The Mathematics of Truth and Beauty,* by K.C. Cole, Harcourt Brace & Co., New York, 1998

George Gilder: "Happy Birthday Wired," by George Gilder, *Wired,* Jan. 1998

Danny Hillis: "The Big Picture," by Danny Hillis, *Wired,* Jan. 1998

Jaron Lanier: "Taking Stock," by Jaron Lanier, *Wired,* Jan. 1998

Kevin Kelley: "New Rules for the New Economy," by Kevin Kelley, *Wired,* Sept. 1997

Ed Rasala, Tracy Kidder: *The Soul of a New Machine,* by Tracy Kidder, Avon Books, New York, 1995.

Pink Floyd: "Breathe," *The Dark Side of the Moon,* lyrics by Roger Waters, TRO-Hampshire House Publishing Corp., 1973.

Bruce Sterling: "Good Cop, Bad Hacker," by Bruce Sterling, *Wired,* May 1995.

Joseph Campbell: *The Power of Myth,* by Joseph Campbell with Bill Moyers, Doubleday, New York, 1988.

Archimedes: *Webster's Ninth New Collegiate Dictionary,* Merriam-Webster Inc., Springfield, Mass., 1986.

Acknowledgments

First thanks go to my parents, Toshio and Sally, who brought me into this world, encouraged me to follow my passion, and continue to watch over me from near and afar, and to my brothers, Rich and Paul, for the bonds that can't be broken.

I'm deeply indebted to those colleagues who so generously gave of their time to teach me their computer tricks: Dan Cowles, Maurice E. Williams, Jeremy Davis, Salvatore Principato, Marc Stern, Jim McMahon, Nick Torello, David Hendrickson, Kiggundu Michael Mukasa. Your teaching helped simplify a complex world and, to this day, helps me make a living.

Big, big thanks to my most supportive agents, Laurie Fox and Linda Chester, who believed in me from the get-go and never fail to show how much they care. I feel incredibly lucky to have you in my corner.

A deep bow as well to my former editor, Mary Ann Naples, who championed my cause two times over, and to my current editor, Geoffrey Kloske, who kept the faith and turned a time of change into a time of opportunity. Thanks also to Nicole Graev for steering the book through, and Katy Riegel for the finishing touches.

Kudos, too, to: Bob Farley and Jeff McDaniel, for sharing their computer tales; my Finnish friend Kimmo Kivelä, for his vision and enthusiasm; Ken "Oneline" Hiratsuka, for the unseen line; Gini Sikes and David Conrad, for thinking to share the computer haiku; Renee Glaser, for her precision and care; Kevin Murakami, for his helpful reading; and my technical editor, Tom Buell, for guarding the book's credibility.

Also in my thoughts: the folks at Apple, Adobe, Quark, who put so much power in the hands of ordinary people like me; and all the techies, hackers, geeks, and visionaries who brought this exciting age into being—I do not take it for granted.

Last, and most important:

to Naomi and Keith, who every day show me why,

and to my true love, Tracy—

my beginning,

my ending,

the 0 to my 1.

$0 = 1$

Author Contact

The author welcomes comments, questions, and inquiries via e-mail at:

psudo@zencomputer.com

or via regular mail at:

Zen Computer
P.O. Box 385278
Minneapolis, MN 55438

All are invited to visit the Zen Computer website at:

http://www.zencomputer.com

T-shirts, recordings of the author's music, and other Zen Computer stuff available by contacting the above.

About the Author

Philip Toshio Sudo is a Japanese-American musician and the author of *Zen Guitar*. His background in Zen comes from extensive study in Eastern philosophy, twelve years living in Japan, and the study of martial arts. He lives with his wife and children in Maui, Hawaii.